HAWTHORNE

THE SCARLET LETTER

NOTES

COLES EDITORIAL BOARD

Bound to stay open

Publisher's Note

Otabind (Ota-bind). This book has been bound using the patented Otabind process. You can open this book at any page, gently run your finger down the spine, and the pages will lie flat.

ABOUT COLES NOTES

COLES NOTES have been an indispensible aid to students on five continents since 1948.

COLES NOTES are available for a wide range of individual literary works. Clear, concise explanations and insights are provided along with interesting interpretations and evaluations.

Proper use of COLES NOTES will allow the student to pay greater attention to lectures and spend less time taking notes. This will result in a broader understanding of the work being studied and will free the student for increased participation in discussions.

COLES NOTES are an invaluable aid for review and exam preparation as well as an invitation to explore different interpretive paths.

COLES NOTES are written by experts in their fields. It should be noted that any literary judgement expressed herein is just that — the judgement of one school of thought. Interpretations that diverge from, or totally disagree with any criticism may be equally valid.

COLES NOTES are designed to supplement the text and are not intended as a substitute for reading the text itself. Use of the NOTES will serve not only to clarify the work being studied, but should enhance the reader's enjoyment of the topic.

ISBN 0-7740-3355-X

© COPYRIGHT 1996 AND PUBLISHED BY
COLES PUBLISHING COMPANY
TORONTO—CANADA
PRINTED IN CANADA

Manufactured by Webcom Limited
Cover finish: Webcom's Exclusive **Duracoat**

CONTENTS

THE SCARLET LETTER

PLOT DIAGRAM

CHAPTERS	1	2	3	4	5	6	7	8	9	10	11	12	13	14	15	16	17	18	19	20	21	22	23	24
HESTER	Ill in prison		Meets lost husband								Joins Dimmesdale on scaffold		Finds courage to hate Chillingworth				Weakens self-confidence attempting to rejoin Dimmesdale						Joins Dimmesdale publicly on scaffold	Returns after travels to live in Salem
CHILLINGWORTH									Delves more deeply into minister's personality as animosity grows			Takes Dimmesdale from scaffold												Tempts Dimmesdale; dies soon after minister
DIMMESDALE							Defends Hester at governor's house					Mounts scaffold at night					Talks to Hester in forest about fleeing						Attempts to publicly confess sin; dies	
PEARL				Chases children teasing her and Hester				Talks back to governor and minister		Calls minister and Chillingworth each 'the Black Man'						Gets angry in forest at minister and changed Hester							Cries at final scaffold scene	Goes to England; marries well
HISTORICAL AND LITERARY TIME	June, 1642. The author says that he begins some 'fifteen or twenty years' after 1630		About two weeks later			Summer, 1645. Pearl is three years old						Early May, 1649, literary time; Historical time is the date of Governor Winthrop's death, March, 1649			Mid-May, 1649, literary time					Last week in May, day in literary time	Early summer, 1649, literary time; same day in June as when literary novel opens			From about 1650 to 1680

THE SCARLET LETTER

SALEM HARBOR

SALEM
KEY MAP

NORTH RIVER

HOUSE OF SEVEN GABLES

TURNER ST.

DERBY ST.

CUSTOM HOUSE

ORANGE ST.

DERBY WHARF

DOCK AREA

HESTER'S HOUSE

SHORE SIDE WHERE HESTER AND PEARL WALKED

HAWTHORNE'S BIRTHPLACE

CHARTER ST. BURYING GROUND

CHARTER ST.

HOUSE OF DIMMESDALE AND CHILLINGWORTH

MARKET PLACE

MALL ST.

MALL ST. HOUSE

SUMMER ST.

WITCH HOUSE

ESSEX ST.

TO BOSTON

THIS MAP, CONJECTURED BY THE WRITER, FRANK O'BRIEN, Ph.D. IS TO SERVE ONLY AS A SOURCE OF REFERENCE.

NATHANIEL HAWTHORNE

DATE	AGE	BIOGRAPHIC HIGHLIGHTS	MAJOR PUBLICATIONS	CONTEMPORARY EVENTS		LITERARY EVENTS	
1804		BORN, JULY 4, SALEM, MASS.		BATTLE OF TRAFALGAR	1805	WEBSTER'S Dictionary	1806
1808	4	FATHER DIES OF YELLOW FEVER		FULTON LAUNCHES 'CLERMONT'	1807	BYRON, The Prisoner of Chillon	1816
1821	17	ENTERS BOWDOIN COLLEGE		FRENCH DEFEATED AT LEIPZIG	1813	J. AUSTEN DIES	1817
1825	21	GRADUATES FROM BOWDOIN		CONGRESS OF VIENNA OPENS	1814	KEATS, The Eve of St. Agnes	1820
1828	24		Fanshawe	KARL MARX BORN	1818	FEODOR DOSTOEVSKY BORN	1821
1837	33		Twice-Told Tales	MONROE DOCTRINE	1823	BEGINNING OF ENGLISH VICTORIAN LITERATURE	1832
1838	34	ENGAGED TO SOPHIA PEABODY		JACKSON ELECTED PRESIDENT	1828	THACKERAY, Vanity Fair	1846
1839	35	APPOINTED TO BOSTON CUSTOM HOUSE		McCORMICK INVENTS 'REAPER'	1834	DUMAS, FILS, VOLUME OF VERSE	1847
1841	37	JOINS BROOK FARM		BATTLE OF ALAMO	1836	POE, Annabel Lee	1849
1842	38	MARRIES SOPHIA PEABODY		MORSE INVENTS TELEGRAPH	1837	DICKENS, David Copperfield	1849
1846	42		Mosses from an Old Manse	TCHAIKOVSKY BORN	1840	BEGINNINGS OF FRENCH REALISM	1850's
1850	46	MOVES TO FARM IN BERKSHIRES	The Scarlet Letter	TEXAS BECOMES STATE	1845	TENNYSON NAMED POET LAUREATE	1850
1851	47		House of Seven Gables	COMMUNIST MANIFESTO	1848	MELVILLE, Moby Dick	1852
1852	48	BUYS 'THE WAYSIDE' IN CONCORD	The Blithedale Romances	CALIFORNIA GOLD RUSH	1849	STOWE, Uncle Tom's Cabin	1852
1853	49	APPOINTED U. S. CONSUL, LIVERPOOL	Tanglewood Tales	NAPOLEON BECOMES EMPEROR	1852	THOREAU, Walden	1854
1858	54	TRAVELS EUROPEAN CONTINENT		CRIMEAN WAR ENDS	1856	WHITMAN, Leaves of Grass	1855
1860	56	RETURNS TO 'WAYSIDE'	The Marble Faun	LINCOLN AND DOUGLAS DEBATE	1858	BAUDELAIRE, Flowers of Evil	1857
1861	57		BEGINS Dr. Grimshawe's Secret	DARWIN'S Origin of Species	1859	ELIOT, Adam Bede	1859
1863	59		BEGINS The Dolliver Romance	AMERICAN CIVIL WAR BEGINS	1861	HUGO, Les Miserables	1862
1864	60	DIES, MAY 19, PLYMOUTH, N. H.		KU KLUX KLAN FORMED	1866	THACKERAY DIES	1863

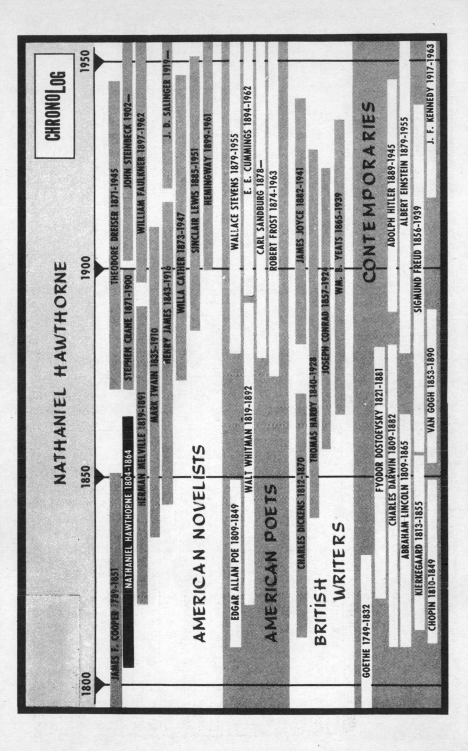

CHRONOLOG

NATHANIEL HAWTHORNE

1800   1850   1900   1950

JAMES F. COOPER 1789-1851
NATHANIEL HAWTHORNE 1804-1864
HERMAN MELVILLE 1819-1891
THEODORE DREISER 1871-1945
STEPHEN CRANE 1871-1900
WILLIAM FAULKNER 1897-1962
JOHN STEINBECK 1902—
MARK TWAIN 1835-1910
HENRY JAMES 1843-1916
WILLA CATHER 1873-1947
SINCLAIR LEWIS 1885-1951
HEMINGWAY 1899-1961
J. D. SALINGER 1919—

AMERICAN NOVELISTS

EDGAR ALLAN POE 1809-1849
WALT WHITMAN 1819-1892
WALLACE STEVENS 1879-1955
E. E. CUMMINGS 1894-1962
CARL SANDBURG 1878—
ROBERT FROST 1874-1963

AMERICAN POETS

CHARLES DICKENS 1812-1870
THOMAS HARDY 1840-1928
JOSEPH CONRAD 1857-1924
JAMES JOYCE 1882-1941
WM. B. YEATS 1865-1939

BRITISH
WRITERS

GOETHE 1749-1832
CHOPIN 1810-1849
KIERKEGAARD 1813-1855
ABRAHAM LINCOLN 1809-1865
CHARLES DARWIN 1809-1882
FYODOR DOSTOEVSKY 1821-1881
VAN GOGH 1853-1890
SIGMUND FREUD 1856-1939
ALBERT EINSTEIN 1879-1955
ADOLPH HITLER 1889-1945
J. F. KENNEDY 1917-1963

CONTEMPORARIES

BIOGRAPHY

Nathaniel Hawthorne was born in Salem, Massachusetts, July 4, 1804, the son of a merchant captain, who died when the boy was only four years old. When he was twelve, his mother took him to live with her brother in Raymond, Maine. A leg injury in childhood severely crippled him for several years, and during this period he developed a habit of solitude and a taste for reading that was to remain with him in varying intensity for the rest of his life. With the generous help of relatives, Hawthorne attended Bowdoin College (1821—1825) in Brunswick, Maine. At college he became friendly with Longfellow, Franklin Pierce (later fourteenth President of the United States), and Horatio Bridge, who later subsidized the first printing of *Twice Told Tales*. Hawthorne's college years seem only remarkable for their normality, and we must not take his word that he was "an idle student." He continued to read widely and left school with no greater blot on his record than being fined fifty cents on one occasion for gambling. He left school also with the firm conviction that he was to be a writer.

Hawthorne regarded the years from 1825—1837 at his mother's house in Salem as a period of haunted and dreamy solitude, but he was, nonetheless, active in his writing. In 1828 he published anonymously his first novel, *Fanshawe*, an unhappily conceived chronicle of life at Bowdoin. The work was so obviously a failure that Hawthorne recalled the work and destroyed as many copies as he could gather. Hawthorne, during this period, made many walking tours of the more remote parts of New England with the aid of an uncle who had a well-established stage coach business. Continuing to contribute to Christmas annuals and various magazines, he edited in 1836 a short-lived periodical for Samuel Griswold Goodrich (1793—1860). In 1837, *Twice Told Tales*, Hawthorne's first great collection of stories, was published; it was enlarged in 1842. His genius had been noted in the London *Athenaeum*, but recognition in America was slow in coming. In fact, at no time in his life were his book sales sufficient to support himself and his family.

In 1838 he was secretly engaged to Sophia Peabody, a Salem neighbor and the descendant of another distinguished Massachusetts family. In 1838 the historian George Bancroft. then collector of the port of Boston, appointed him to the Boston Custom House, a job he held until 1841. In that last year he tried several months of socialist—communal living at Brook Farm near Boston in the hopes that he would somehow find it easier to support a wife in the environment. However, it was soon obvious that the plan was as uncomfortable as it was unlikely, and upon his marriage in 1842 Hawthorne settled at the Old Manse, Ralph Waldo Emerson's family home in Concord, Massachusetts. Hawthorne's mixed feelings towards the Brook Farm experiment are demonstrated in *The Blithedale Romance* (1852). The four years at Concord in semi-retirement were happy ones for the Hawthornes. His pen, though active, was not golden in the financial sense. He issued *Biographical Studies* (1842) for children and wrote sketches and studies for the *Democratic Review* which formed the *Mosses from an Old Manse* (1846).

The *Review* failed, and when Hawthorne lost a portion of his savings in Brook Farm, he was again forced to accept another custom house job —this time as a surveyor in Salem. The details of the years (1846—1849) at this post are elaborated in "The Custom House" section later analyzed here. It is clear that the job gave Hawthorne pause for his masterpiece, *The Scarlet Letter* (1850), which was published the year after he lost his appointment. Hawthorne was stimulated by the book's reception, and soon after he published two other novels, *The House of Seven Gables* (1851) and *The Blithdale Romance* (1852) along with *A Wonder Book* (1852), a collection of Greek myths for children which ranks high in the canon of juvenile classics.

It was in this most fruitful period, while temporarily staying in the Berkshires, that Hawthorne met Herman Melville (1819—1891). Although they were not in close contact for very long, the men were friendly. The older Hawthorne made such a forceful impression on the writer of sea stories that *Moby Dick* (1851) was re-cast in its present form as a partial consequence of this association and of Melville's reading of *Mosses from an Old Manse*. The senior writer had acted as a catalyst for the cosmic themes so long held in the mind of Melville. Hawthorne settled at the Wayside in Concord in 1852 and wrote a life of General Franklin Pierce, his college friend. On his inauguration as President in 1853, Pierce named Hawthorne consul at Liverpool, a job he held for over four years. Hawthorne was not completely at ease in this work, but he carried his obligations conscientiously. After this the Hawthornes sojourned for nearly two years in Rome and Florence. These travels supplied him with the materials for *The Marble Faun* (1860).

Returning to Concord in June of 1860, Hawthorne wrote some superb articles on English life for the *Atlantic Monthly,* later collected as *Our Old Home* (1863). He died four years later while on a carriage expedition in New Hampshire with his old friend Pierce. Hawthorne was just short of sixty and had merited a reputation which has never ceased growing. He was active to the very end, and during the period 1860—1864 he had labored with four romances, all unfinished in varying degrees: *The Ancestral Footstep, Dr. Grimshawe's Secret, Septimius Felton,* and *The Dolliver Romance.* His family and relatives did much in their way to promulgate his reputation or what they thought should be his reputation. In this last instance, it took the critics some years before they realized his wife had contributed a great deal to an erroneous image of the man by her timid tinkering with Hawthorne's notebooks.

* * * * * * * * * * * *

"Where Hawthorne is known, he seems to be deemed a pleasant writer, with a pleasant style—a sequestered, harmless man, from whom any deep and weighty thing would hardly be anticipated: a man who means no meanings. But there is no man, in whom humor and love, like mountain peaks, soar to such a rapt height as to receive the irradiations of the upper skies; there is no man in whom humor and love are developed in that high form called genius—no such man can exist without also possessing, as the indispensable complement of these, a great, deep intellect which drops down into the universe like a plummet . . . .

"In one word, the world is mistaken in this Nathaniel Hawthorne. He himself must often have smiled at its absurd misconception of him. He is immeasurably deeper than the plummet of the mere critic. For it is not the brain that can test such a man; it is only the heart. You cannot come to know greatness by inspecting it; there is no glimpse to be caught of it, except by intuition; you need not ring it, you but touch it, and you find it is gold.

"Now it is that blackness in Hawthorne, of which I have spoken, that so fixes and fascinates me. It may be, nevertheless, that it is too largely developed in him. Perhaps he does not give us a ray of his light for every shade of his dark. But however this may be, this blackness it is that furnishes the infinite obscure of his background—that background, against which Shakespeare plays his grandest conceits, the things that have made for Shakespeare his loftiest but most circumscribed renown, as the profoundest of thinkers."

–Herman Melville from "Hawthorne and His Mosses"

INTRODUCTION

Nathaniel Hawthorne was a writer with antiquarian interests, who had the desire for seclusion that craft encourages, and a man very much a public figure in his day who had a sense of public service. At various times he seemed as much concerned with the unsolvable presence and effects of evil in individual man as he was at other times involved with the improvement of the commonweal. *The Scarlet Letter* demonstrates the effects of these various attractions. Almost every major character in the work suffers or is affected by an interior sense of sin, and several of the characters who function as public figures or who act as symbols for the community show how individual action mitigates the public welfare or changes common opinion. *The Scarlet Letter* is not merely the study of a singular fall from grace; it is an artistic elaboration of how one sin or flaw affects not only the participants but also the onlookers. It is also a presentation of the decline of an enclosed society. Equally it demonstrates science's effect upon a body of religious belief and the awesome effects of religious conviction on the individual as a member of a community.

To truly appreciate the elaborate richness of Hawthorne's novel, one must work as he did from the interior mentality outwards and from the factually probable to the fancifully pertinent. Hawthorne thought long and hard upon the theme of his first and greatest masterpiece. In "Endicott and the Red Cross" (1837), referring to various people punished by the authorities in seventeenth-century Salem, the narrator mentions "a young woman, with no mean share of beauty, whose doom it was to wear the letter "A" on the breast of her gown, in the eyes of all the world and her own children . . . sporting with her infamy, the lost and desperate creature had embroidered the fatal token in scarlet cloth, with golden thread and the nicest art of needle work; so that the capital "A" might have been thought to mean Admirable or anything rather than Adulteress."

But for the reference to more than one child, this is the Hester Prynne so nobly drawn in 1850. A few years after the mention of the adulteress in the short story, Hawthorne jotted the following item in one of his notebooks: "the life of a woman who by an old (Plymouth) law, was condemned always to wear the letter "A" sewed on her garment in token of her having committed adultery." A short time after, probably thinking further on how to elaborate his story, he noted his interest in writing "a story of the effects of revenge, diabolizing him who indulges in it." This, of course, is the transformation wrought in and by Roger Chillingworth, Hester's physically and emotionally crippled husband.

These are a few of the things which show Hawthorne's creative imagination at work, and they provide guidelines for one's own analysis. However, as will be seen in "The Custom House," Hawthorne was encouraged in his fancy by the promptings of history. *The Scarlet Letter* begins at one time and place and then explodes to universal significance as it proceeds. In the Salem court records for 1688 is mentioned the punishment of one Hester Crawford, who was publicly whipped for having an affair with John Wadg. Hawthorne probably knew of this, not only because of his insatiable interests in colonial history, but because his first American ancestor, William Hathorne, was charged with supervising the execution of that sentence. One other piece of information in the records encourages this probability: Hester was to be punished "a month or six weeks after the birth of a child."

Here then are all of the major ingredients for the tale of the infamous and famous letter: secret sin and public scorn and personal tragedy which becomes somehow admirable.

COMPLETE BACKGROUND

Puritans — Puritanism

To give a complete description of Puritanism would be to give a cultural history of colonial New England. However, a few points should be made clear to inhibit the generalities ordinarily associated with these terms. The word was suggested by the Latin *puritas,* purity. In American history the Puritans were an early manifestation of the Congregational Church who, like the later body, felt that the English Church in its various forms had not separated sufficiently in rite and dogma from the Church of Rome. Hence the Puritans are often called separatists.

The Puritans who came to America around 1628 were men who were escaping the restrictions and prohibitions of the Anglican Church. They were not poverty-stricken exiles, criminals, or bondservants. They were extremely conscious of their national heritage but had greater devotion to their individual consciences. They wished to be free to worship in their fashion. Unfortunately and illogically, as soon as some of them in their various congregations attained power in the New World, they insisted that others conform or face exile or other punishments. In short, for many Church and State were one.

It is difficult to pin-point specific views held in common by the many independent Puritan or separatist churches. However, they did insist on a personal often ecstatic communion with their Godhead and generally were suspicious of any elaborate hierarchial order. They emphasized the plain life and hard work and in general the equality of all men under God provided those men had assented to God's supremacy in a fashion congenial to their religious views. The central idea was the sanctity of the Church members *per se,* rather than that of the ministry as a clerical order. Harvard College (1636) and Yale College (1701) were founded by the Congregationalists (the more general title) as seminaries. America owes them much, for without their moral sense (as dark as it may have been for some) and their concern for equality under law our nation would not be what it is.

History of Early Salem

The name Salem was quite popular with the colonials, and there are easily four other well-known and still-flourishing communities that chose this name at their inception in the period before 1850. Salem is the ancient name for Jeru*salem* and, aside from connoting the religious orientation of the American settlers, it also suggests their optimism looking for a new world with new beginning. The irony of this optimism in conjunction with Hawthorne's novel is that the Puritans brought their old-world sense of sin into their new Jerusalem. The locale for our tale was settled in 1626 by Roger Conant (1593—1679) and a group of planters who had made an earlier try at Cape Ann. Originally, Salem was a commercial enterprise, in part for agricultural reasons and partly to have a shelter for men who fished off the coastal region in the harsh winter months.

In 1628 a small company under the jurisdiction of Governor John Endicott was given a patent for the territory by the New England Council to the Dorchester Company. This was the first group to arrive with intentions of a permanent settlement. Another charter for the Massachusetts Bay Colony was issued in 1629 to supersede the previous patent. Endicott continued as governor until John Winthrop arrived in 1630. He eventually removed the seat of government to Boston.

By this time the settlement had assumed the religious character Hawthorne employs in his novel. In fact, in August 1629 the first Congregational Church in America was established here; its pastor for those early years was Roger Williams, a friend of Endicott. He was always popular in Salem but had to flee in 1635 to Rhode Island to avoid arrests by Massachusetts Bay officials. In 1692 Salem Village was thrown into an uproar about the alleged presence of witches and black magic. The delusion spread, and in that period occurred the famous witch-hunt in which hundreds of colonials were arrested and many tried; nineteen were hanged and one was squeezed to death. Tradition has it that the hangings took place on what is now called Gallows Hill near Salem.

While it is easy to conjure the fault as typical of that cliche' called the Puritan mentality, it should be noted that the punishments were executed in the form prescribed by English law. In the British Isles, there were many capital punishments executed long after the Salem hysteria had died out. Nonetheless it should be clear that the diabolical atmosphere of Hawthorne's novel and the quick assumptions of various minor characters that "The Black Man" was abroad and walking has more than a casual connection to the mentality of Salem folk in the period.

Historical and Literary Time in The Scarlet Letter

Although he infers specific dates at places in the action, Hawthorne did not wish to strongly suggest an exact and constant span of years in the novel with respect to the progress of actual events in Salem history. Nonetheless, realize that a factual span of history gives dimension to the novel. Despite hints that all takes place "some fifteen or twenty years later" than 1630, the novel's action begins in 1642 and ends in 1649 (if we exclude the time of Pearl's marriage and Hester's final return). In Chapter XII Hawthorne mentions that Hester ministered at the death-bed of Governor Winthrop. The time of year, "early May," seems deliberately inaccurate, since such a researcher as Hawthorne must have known it took place in March. Nonetheless, the year was 1649, and once we realize that, many things fall into place. Hawthorne says also there that it has been "seven long years" since the first scaffold scene. In point of historical fact, Governor Richard Bellingham ended his first term of office in 1642, and since in the novel he had publicly addressed Hester on her day of shame, the times fit neatly. We are told further that the last sequence of events (Chapters XXI–XXIII) happens on a single day seven years after the time of the first chapter, and by textual evidence this would mean early summer, still in 1649.

Pearl is three years old in Chapters VII and VIII, and the time would be 1645, when Bellingham was serving as magistrate or deputy governor (not governor) as Hawthorne suggests in the opening paragraph of Chapter VIII. She is seven at the time of the second scaffold scene as has been stated above, and, having reached the traditional age of reason, Pearl acts a foil to the minister who is on the brink of insanity. (Realizing her age, by the way, is another strong indication of her precocious-ness in the bold conversation she carries on with Bellingham in Chapter VII).

In Chapter XIII we witness Hester's change to a world of speculation, and, as has been stated, we see some good come from her tragedy. Hawthorne says, "she might have come down to us in history, hand in hand with Ann Hutchinson, as the foundress of a religious sect." The irony of this compliment is that Ann Hutchinson at this time (1649) had been six years in her grave after being banished from Massachusetts by its clergy and later murdered by Indians in New York.

Chillingworth's death takes place within the year of Dimmesdale's confession and fatal collapse. The time would be towards the close of 1649. One can answer then that Hester and Pearl left on their travels of "many years" very near the year 1650. If Pearl were about eight when they left and about eighteen when she married, she would be settling in post-Cromwellian England or at least at a time when the English were about to return their homage to the monarchy.

Hester receives letters from Pearl which are marked with "armorial seals upon them, though of bearings unknown to English heraldry." The suggestion seems strong enough that Pearl has not gone from one Puritan government to another, rather she has left that heritage behind her to participate in the often cynical, but nonetheless rationalistic and scientific climate which began in the court of Charles II in 1660. Pearl, unlike Hester, has managed to travel to a new time and place, one in which her mother would never find comfort. Roger Chillingworth, the satanic rationalist and scientist, has not only given Pearl his financial estate, he has also bequeathed Pearl the Age of Reason glorified by Sir Isaac Newton (1642–1727), Robert Boyle (1627–1691), and John Locke (1632–1704). The motto of Charles' scientists and cavalier sophisticates was "on no one's word." From what we have seen of young Pearl, she would be an apt member of such a society.

CAPSULE SUMMARY

Hester Prynne, a lovely and fiery Salem woman, is discovered by that community to be an adultress. She is brought to trial and sentenced to wear a scarlet letter "A" on her bosom as punishment. The sentence is light because of Hester's age, the baby girl she has given birth to while in prison, and because it is not known whether Hester's husband lives. Hester's shame has been made that much more intense because she has refused to name her partner in the love affair, and she alone must bare the gossip and stares of a spiteful community.

While confined in prison to fulfill another part of the punishment, Hester is visited by her secretly returned husband, who has taken the name Roger Chillingworth. Chillingworth, with the knowledge of medicine learned in England and from his Indian captors, cures Hester and her daughter Pearl of a nervous malady which had infected their entire physical beings. He makes Hester promise that she will not reveal his identity, and it is obvious from his manner that he will use this disguise to discover Hester's partner in love.

The unknown man is Roger Dimmesdale, a well-respected and loved young minister in the community, and he and Hester pass in quiet anguish as she again takes up life in Salem. Hester earns a living by sewing and embroidery; her best work seems to be spent on the elfin and angel-like girl, Pearl, who senses the shame attached to the scarlet letter even in infancy. Hester slowly grows to a new woman, one who works great charities for an unforgiving neighborhood; Pearl grows to childhood with ever-increasing sauciness and precocity; and as all this happens, the doctor and the minister drift closer together.

Chillingworth is a needed addition to Salem; some of the citizens see in him not only a good doctor but one who might cure Dimmesdale of the strange weakness that grows on him daily. One day after the two men have taken up residence together, the minister falls into sudden sleep after a heated discussion over sin and confession with Chillingworth. The wily doctor creeps to the minister's room and there, after uncovering his chest, sees or thinks he sees a scarlet letter "A" on the flesh of the minister.

From now on, the tortures of the minister are more severe than ever. In a forest walk with Pearl, Hester tells Dimmesdale the identity of the doctor, and they then agree to leave Salem with Pearl and seek a new life. As a sign of her determination, Hester loosens her hair and throws down the shamefilled symbol, but Pearl, shocked at the great change in her mother and distrustful of Dimmesdale, insists that Hester dress as before. Hester consents, but she and Dimmesdale still make their plans to leave.

On Election Day several years after Hester's public shame, the minister mounts the same scaffold that Hester had and confesses his guilt in the adultery. As he does so, he calls the mother and child to his side, and he dies moments later broken by fear, shame, and the great anguish intensified by Chillingworth, who even now, on the same scaffold, attempts to prolong Dimmesdale's agony.

The crowd, expecting an ordinary sermon on this usually festive occasion, is thrown into an uproar by the scene before them. Even now, many of them are still too hardhearted to forgive Hester or too respectful of the false reputation of Dimmesdale to believe what they hear. Their own opinions are bolstered in a variety of ways because of their previous convictions and because Dimmesdale's remarks are not as blunt as his anguish could have made them. Even in dying Dimmesdale is not so brave as to teach and tell the truth straight out. Chillingworth also dies within the year and leaves Pearl a considerable estate. She and Hester travel for some years, and the young girl finally settles in England where she marries well. Hester, who has returned to Salem to live out her remaining years, dies in all the sorrow of her years and is buried next to Dimmesdale.

COMPREHENSIVE SUMMARY

The Custom House: Introductory

The prefatory chapter to *The Scarlet Letter* tells, in a rather discursive fashion, of Hawthorne's three-year service in the Salem Custom House and of some of the venerable but sleepy old men who fell under his command. One cannot escape the relaxed mood of the quiet warfside, the respectable-looking and dilapidated brick custom house, and the torpor of its inhabitants because the narrator's style is so relaxed. When Hawthorne tells us towards the end of the chapter that he has discovered by accident a decayed embroidered "A" and some documents telling of its history and the story of one Hester Prynne, belief comes easily. We have been prepared for something factually true. By mixing fact and fiction, Hawthorne has managed to intimate that all that follows "The Custom House" is pertinent to the world of the living.

To see how the chapter works one must separate fact and fiction. Salem was Hawthorne's birthplace and, as he mentions, he had been in and out of it several times before he was appointed Surveyor of the Revenue (1846-1849). (He held the post until the election of President Zachary Taylor on the Whig ticket in 1848 led to his replacement.) Maritime trade was ebbing in the mid-nineteenth century, and there is every reason to believe that his working day was as unrushed as he says. The work, or lack of it, was a needed change from intellectually communal life of Brook Farm and the associations with Ralph Waldo Emerson and Henry David Thoreau. Although the narrator does not mention him by name, his claim to Salem extends to one of its first settlers. William Hathorne, "soldier, legislator, judge," had emigrated from England in 1630. He and his son John both had "the persecuting spirit," and the latter was a judge in the famous (or infamous) Salem witchcraft trials of 1692. When Nathaniel says that he takes shame upon himself and asks that any curse incurred by them may be now and henceforth removed, there is nothing fictional in the sentiment. The tale that follows is part of that expiation.

Hawthorne spends nearly a third of this chapter discussing the elderly civil servants he met in his service at Salem. What he is doing, of course, is gradually leading us back in time. The men are all existing in the present, but their world is of the past; they tell well-worn anecdotes of times long gone; the Inspector recollects "the good dinners which had no small portion of the happiness of his life to eat;" and the Collector of Customs, "our gallant old General," dreams of the times he led the bayonets at Chippewa or Fort Erie.

The time is now ripe for a more personal and more fanciful return to the first reason for this prefatory chapter — to prepare us for the 'discovery' of the scarlet letter and its story. Hawthorne, speaking in the role of a story teller and not as the true descendant of Salem witchhunters, mentions that literary concerns had no interest for him as he immersed himself in the hum-drum existence of a civil servant. He wishes us to think that he has no extraordinary stake in what follows.

To pass the time, he rummages in the upper story of the custom house, and there amidst dusty and decaying records he finds the embroidered letter and its documents: "I happened to place it on my breast. It seemed to me, — the reader may smile, but must not doubt my word, — it seemed to me, then that I experienced a sensation not altogether physical, yet almost so, as of burning heat, and so if the letter were not of red cloth, but red-hot iron." The construction of this statement illustrates how easily Hawthorne, the literary artist, has drawn us into the world of the imagination. He insists that we not doubt him; what he discovered is as real as his Salem ancestry. Yet, the burning sensation *seemed* to be felt; at least *then* such *seemed* the case; it was not "altogether physical, yet almost so."

The series of qualifications, a device often used by Hawthorne, allows the narrator to vacillate from the factually probable to the fanciful. To bolster the illusion of the reality of discovery, Hawthorne mentions that the documents were in the hand of one Surveyor Pue, a man who had actually held Hawthorne's post in the mid-eighteenth century. Jonathan Pue's own working hours were long with inactivity, and he had researched this episode from the earlier century. All that Hawthorne claims is the role of editor: what Pue leaves unsaid, Hawthorne creates to suit the probable circumstances. When he finally does leave the post that had become more and more stultifying, Hawthorne is free to carry out what he imagines would have been the injunction of Surveyor Pue had he met the ghost in some dusty corner of the custom house: "Do this . . . do this, and the profit shall be your own." The profit is as much ours as it was Hawthorne's. Now the living room of his house becomes the "neutral territory somewhere between the real world and fairy land, where the Actual and the Imaginary may meet, and each imbues itself with the nature of the other."

While this preamble may seem to cover large and widely different aspects of Hawthorne's life, real and imagined, it is unified totally by the character of our narrator. Moreover, the chapter fits well within the literary mainstream. Many romance writers, as Hawthorne enjoyed calling himself, anchored their stories in the real world by referring to actual events or places. Many of the novels we still enjoy reading were claimed to have been found in attics, diaries, or journals of persons whom the 'editors' claimed to have known. The device brings verisimilitude to the work and gives the artist great latitude in creating the unusual, which in turn is passed off as factual. When Hawthorne claims to present a story outlined by a man living a century before him, who in turn had investigated the previous century, the events are not only bolstered by the decayed but still extant scarlet letter, but also the reader is given a frame of vision and very specified points of reference. We are prepared to accept the story as possible even though our 'editor' has interpolated events such as a specific conversation and the state of a character's mind at any one moment which (he would claim) have been lost, omitted, or distorted along the way. Hawthorne may claim that the dialogues are his own, but that the love affair, the demonic husband, and anguished death of Dimmesdale — as well as the 'magic' of Hester's "A" — are all factually true; he has the embroidery to prove it!

For some, "The Custom House" may seem bleak on first reading. The old men, although gently treated, are obviously in their dotage and most are little more than vegetables with memories. Salem does not lend itself, even in Hawthorne's day, to the forthrightly jovial response; and the earlier Salem with its supposed witches, and the Bible and sword morality of its inhabitants may seem formidably somber. However, our narrator does have a sense of humor, and this makes the ghostly tale, the burning letter, and the present tedium of custom house life easy to bear. When Hawthorne tells of his dismissal, he pokes fun at his own political martyrdom: "I had won the crown of martyrdom, though with no longer a head to bear it on." The imaginary ghost of Pue, which demands that the tale be written, also demands in comic fashion more than casual mention: "I charge you, in this matter of old Mistress Prynne, give to your predecessor's memory the credit which will be rightfully its due!" Hawthorne's sense of humor acts as more than a dramatic pause. It also shows that the present descendant of a long line of morally serious Puritans is of a different day and different beliefs. The humor presumes that he is not out to convince the reader of anything. He is to portray events as they happened. Paradoxically, the humor only fortifies the coming horrors.

I. The Prison Door   A throng of women and bearded men in somber looking clothing wait outside Salem prison at the market place. Although the building was built twenty years after the founding of the settlement, it seems as ancient as time. Bushes of weeds and thorn-apple cluster, like the crowd, around the building. The only contrast to this setting is a wild rose bush. Legend has it that it sprang up under the footsteps of Ann Hutchinson, a religious leader banished for her unorthodox religious views.

COMMENTARY: This chapter, though only three paragraphs, poses the conflict for the rest of the novel. Sin or a sense of sin and the rigors of orthodoxy are as old as time itself, and as powerful as the weather-stained oaken door. However, passionate belief in self and anti-orthodoxy seem just as ageless, and, if not always as powerful, they are at least as hardy. The rose bush and the mention of Ann Hutchinson are introductory suggestions to the fiery and stubborn Hester Prynne, who is soon to leave the prison house.

II. The Market Place   The women begin gossiping as they wait. What is most impressive about their collective character is their coarse physiques and bold speech. Many are dissatisfied with the lightness of Hester's sentence. For her adultery she is to wear a scarlet letter on the bodice of her dress. She is not to be put to death or branded as stated in Scripture or the Puritan Statute-book. Hester's exit from the prison silences everyone, and she stands momentarily before the crowd with a three-month-old infant in her arms. It is obvious that she is different from the other women in more ways than the nature of the crime suggests. She is tall and ladylike and even her clothing is different and shows the recklessness of her nature. What stands out above all else is the fantastically embroidered and illuminated scarlet letter.

As haughty as her demeanor is, Hester is terrified by the sternness of the crowd as she moves towards the pillory scaffold on which she must stand as part of her punishment. Hester's only escape from the leaden stare of the mob is to remember fonder times. Momentarily, at least, she dreams of her native village in England, the faces of her now-dead parents and her own face as a younger and happier girl. One of these memories does not seem as pleasant as the rest. She pictures a man well stricken in years, pale, thin, and scholar-like with a slightly deformed back. The man's eyes, though weakened by much reading, seem to be able to penetrate souls. The present forces itself in again, and she hugs the child so fiercely that it cries out. Only the infant and the shame are real.

COMMENTARY: While the first chapter establishes the forces in a symbolic sense, this one, in a wide sweep of the camera's eye, establishes or mentions all of the major characters. The Reverend Master Dimmesdale stands silent and trembling in the crowd; what we hear from the gossiping women is that he has been grievously hurt by the scandal. We will soon know how much irony that remark holds. Hester's temporary escape into the past is a facile and convenient literary device to sketch her biography, and as she works her thoughts to the present, the image of a "misshapen scholar" introduces the other important man in her life and completes the triangle. This scaffold scene is one of three in the novel, and at each such scene something shocking and important will happen.

III. The Recognition   Two strangers stand on the edge of the crowd facing the scaffold. One is an Indian; the other, in a strange disarray of civilized and savage costume, is the misshapen and scholarly-looking man Hester has been thinking about. Although seemingly uninterested in what is going on before him, a writhing horror twists itself across his features in convulsive anger. Just as Hester recognizes him and seems about to show her reaction to the crowd, he calmly raises his finger and lays it to his lips. And then with what seems to be great self-control he begins asking a man in the crowd the background of the culprit and her crime.

We learn that Hester refuses to name her lover and that because of her youth and the possibility her husband may be dead she has been spared the death penalty. As the stranger leaves with his Indian companion, he says, as much to himself as to the Salem citizen, that the girl's lover will be found out. In the manner in which it is said, it carries all of the severity of an oath. As the two move through the crowd, Hester's public inquisition begins. The Reverend John Wilson, after a few pleas for Hester's confession, turns to young Master Dimmesdale, a fellow religious, and asks that he continue the exhortation.

Dimmesdale is as different from the crowd before Hester as she is. His speech is marked with eloquence and religious fervour, his eyes are touched with melancholy, and his skin seems as white as parchment. Notwithstanding his scholarly attainments, there is an air about the man suggestive of a frightened and tremulous angel. So powerful seem the minister's appeals that the people believe for the moment that Hester will name her seducer. The question leads to nothing and another clergyman begins a sermon on sin lasting well over an hour. Over and over again he refers to the scarlet "A", and the embroidery on Hester's dress seems lit with Hell-fire. Only one person, Hester's infant, seems to object to the proceedings; all through the latter part of her mother's ordeal, she screams and writhes in her mother's arms.

COMMENTARY: Another contrast is offered in this chapter. The satanic and scholarly-looking stranger is posed against the angelic and almost effeminate-looking Dimmesdale. Within this contrast the narrator manages to weave many verbal ironies. Whatever the stranger says is true enough, but we will soon realize that it is truth tainted with infernal spite. Hester's seducer will be uncovered, but not for the moral purposes the stranger's comments suggest. Dimmesdale's remarks are also morally valid; as he himself says, Hester's stubbornness shows wondrous strength and generosity in protecting her lover. Dimmesdale in his pleading says that she disregard whatever reputation the man may have, for he (the lover) is as guilty as she. All quite true, and, as we discover, all apply in full force to Dimmesdale, the yet-to-be-discovered partner. Dimmesdale's reactions to his remarks and Hester's quiet refusals are as much an assessment of his own guilt as they are a reflection of his fear of being discovered. The ambivalence of his remarks symbolically project the forces, guilt and fear, conscience and hypocrisy, that will rip his personality in two when he falls prey to the probing and insane nature of the stranger.

Hester's child, in all its reactions, refuses to be part of solemnity, and this is another theme to be developed in the course of the tale. As we watch the child grow to maturity, we realize that she by birth and disposition is never a citizen of Salem. Like Hawthorne's own children, mentioned in "The Custom House," this child will strike her roots in unaccustomed earth, not in the worn-out soil of Salem.

IV. The Interview   Hester is returned to prison to complete her sentence.
It is discovered that she is in such a nervous state that she has to be watched lest (her jailers fear) she commit suicide or hurt the infant. The stranger introduces himself as Roger Chillingworth, a physician, and they allow him to attend Hester and her child who is so overwrought with the tense atmosphere that it is having convulsions. Hester and Chillingworth are left alone, and their conversation gradually reveals that this misshapen alchemist is Hester's missing husband. The medicine that he offers Hester cures both her and the child, but it is offered with such bitterness that Hester fears for a moment that it is poisoned. Chillingworth, however, convinces her that he seeks revenge on the man who has violated his marriage and seduced his wife. In the manner that he makes his vow to uncover her one-time lover, Chillingworth gives the impression that he can read the thoughts of others, and his sensibility seems as diabolic as his intent. Before leaving her cell he insists that she keep his identity a secret.

COMMENTARY: The last few sentences in this chapter pose a difficulty.
It seems strange that Hester would agree to keep her husband's identity when the promise can only result in the even-

tual unmasking of Dimmesdale. In purely human terms, Hester may have been so terrified by Chillingworth that she consented almost hypnotically. Hester may have also realized that if her husband were found alive she might be put to death and her child given to this man's charge. Whatever the reason, Hester's consent evidences a change in her character, for she has now somehow and in some small way aligned herself with vindictive morality. Hester is not a saint, she is a human being; she has made one mistake by falling in love with such a weak man as Dimmesdale, and here she makes another mistake. There is no suggestion that it is done in malice, but it is an injudicious act nonetheless.

From the way the portrayal of Chillingworth is handled it is difficult to sympathize with him. But in the interview he gives several good reasons why his antagonism is partially valid. He was much older than Hester when they married and given to the quiet books rather than the vivacity of youth. He did love Hester in his fashion, or at least he tried. What a shock it must have been to finally work himself from Indian captivity to freedom only to find his wife an adulteress. His anguish is further intensified when he finds his wife with a child that he himself could never have given her. Even Hester admits in the interview that she has wronged this man. Because Hawthorne here and later in the tale concentrates on the calculating and satanic vindictiveness of Chillingworth (even his name denotes frigidity) one tends to lose sight of the natural reasons for his actions. Hester is a heroine in fully human terms, not a saint; so too, Chillingworth, as fiery and diabolic as he seems, is nonetheless a man. To realize the success of Hawthorne's work is to realize that the natural and supernatural are acting and interacting together throughout the work in the same way that fact and fancy work in "The Custom House."

V. Hester and Her Needle   Hester's confinement is now at an end, and as she comes forth into the sunshine she realizes that she must bear the malice and the snide remarks that prison has kept from her. She is free to leave Salem, but she decides to live on the fringe of the community. In so doing she chooses to give up her individuality and become the general symbol at which the preacher and moralist might point. To them she is the reality of sin and the butt of all antagonisms. She even suffers insults from the poor folk to whom she has given alms. Her sin and ignominy are the roots which she has now struck in the soil.

She supports herself by embroidery, and her handiwork decorates the cuffs of magistrates, the vestments and draperies of public occasions, baby linen, and burial shrouds. She is never commissioned to embroider bridal veils; the exception indicates the relentless vigor with which society frowns upon her and her sin. The oppressive moral atmosphere and the never-ending remarks about the scarlet letter not only push Hester into a deeper depression but also seem to give her a second sense. She feels that somehow she has been endowed with a sympathetic knowledge of the hidden sin in other hearts. When passing certain venerable-looking magistrates or ministers, she has the impression of being in the presence of evil. Intuitively she feels that certain women, pure in their public reputation, envy her sin and its one-time pleasure. It was said by some that Hester's "A" glowed at night.

COMMENTARY: It is obvious now that Hester has been thoroughly overwhelmed and subjugated by the community's somber sense of guilt. Hester cannot leave for England or other parts of of the New World because she has no way of escaping from the guilt fostered on her. As suggested in the previous chapter, she has aligned herself with a spirituality that is as dreary and doleful as her grey clothing. Hester's tragedy is accomplished even before her lover is discovered: she has been sacrificed. The 'new' woman to come from this experience will eventually become heroic in another way as she works to convert her Salem neighbors to angelic love by her own endless acts of charity. Hawthorne is saying here and elsewhere that no heroic act can leave the actor untouched. And he leaves us to wonder if the sacrifice is worth it. The new Hester is a sympathetic creation, but the lovely and passionate girl of fiery imagination is no more. Her daughter will grow into what had been her mother's role, but the girl is not of Salem's kind.

The hypocrisy of Salem's morality (or of certain types of communal morality) is underscored in natural and supernatural fashion. In so far as the community is willing to use Hester's art to decorate their own pomp and ceremony, so far does it admit that it is in part responsible for the woman's unnecessary agony and the occasions that led her to it. Moreover, if the animosity of the Salemites can transform a woman's spirit, then it is possible that the sense of evil they have given her can let her read evil in an intuitive and possibly supernatural fashion. Hester's embroidery and newly-developed sense are extensions of hypocrisy on two levels.

The closing paragraph contains the same deliberate overqualification that was noted in "The Custom House." The narrator says that only the ignorant said that the letter glowed at night, and their words are not always to be accepted easily. However, he ends with the statement that the letter burned Hester's bosom so deeply (in the metaphoric sense) that it may have been true after all. One should remember this closing remark, for there will be the same sort of deliberate confusion in the concluding chapter over the "A" supposedly branded on the chest of Dimmesdale.

VI. Pearl   The child is named Pearl, because Hester feels that she has been purchased at great price—with all she had. The name expresses the girl's exotic character, not the calm, white, unimpassioned luster that the gem would suggest. Hester furthers the child's unusual nature by dressing her in the most magnificent clothing her own hands can work. The girl's personality is of so many hues that Hester wonders at times if there are many Pearls, and indeed if this infant is her child at all. It would seem that in giving her existence, a great law had been broken and the result was a being whose elements were brilliant and beautiful but in no way cohesive. As she grows, Hester wonders if the child is more elfin than human, for she seems to possess a continual merriment no way influenced by Hester's own sense of guilt. Pearl, even in the cradle, is attracted to the scarlet letter, and as she learns to walk, she amuses herself with gathering handfuls of flowers and flinging them one by one at her mother's bosom.

COMMENTARY: For every action there is a reaction; Pearl is the reaction to the death of Hester's former self. In looking into the child's eyes, Hester imagines that she sees reflected there not her face but the face of some spirit. Hester interprets the reflection as evil and malicious, but it is more probable that it is a reflection of the first Hester, fiery and passionate, which she now no longer recognizes. Indeed Hester's actions in dressing the child with gorgeous dresses indicates that, subconsciously at least, the desire to live as she once did is still there.

VII. The Governor's Hall   Hester goes to Governor Bellingham's mansion ostensibly to deliver a pair of gloves; the real reason in going is to investigate the rumors surrounding her custody of Pearl. Some Salemites feel that Hester is a poor moral influence and that Pearl should be raised elsewhere in the community. Pearl is three years old now, and as always she accompanies her mother on the trip. In her luxurious clothing young Pearl has become the walking symbol of Hester's adultery, or so the community feels. Along the way some children, acting from the spite inculcated by their parents and the ever-present gossip, decide to fling mud on the little girl. Screaming and shouting with all the force of an avenging angel, she scatters the children and with the same swiftness returns smiling to her mother.

Hester and Pearl are admitted to the governor's hall by a bondservant who assumes that the couple are important visitors. As they pass a glittering suit of newly-made armor, Pearl notices that in the distorted reflection the scarlet letter had become so exaggerated and gigantic a part of her mother's image that she seemed almost hidden by it; Hester becomes pre-occupied with the reflection until the child with her usual merriment draws her mother to look at some flowers in the garden outside.

COMMENTARY: This chapter furthers the unusually volatile and varied personality of Pearl. Pearl's reaction to the children is normal enough; she is merely protecting herself and her mother from the malice she senses from everyone in the village. However, the actions in a thematic sense further illustrate that there are other forces at work countering the dour and prudish morality which has so changed Hester. Pearl in her "naughty merriment" may remind Hester of her guilt, but this interpretation of Hester is only a result of her own sense of defeat and isolation. To the reader, Pearl should suggest the joy of living lost in consequence of the Persecution. So far as Pearl reminds her mother of the adultery, so does Pearl remind us of Hester's great penalty.

VIII. The Elf Child and the Minister Amidst a splendor which seems out of place in such an austere community, Hester meets the Governor. With him are the old minister Mr. Wilson, Dimmesdale, and Chillingworth, who seems to have become a fully-accepted member of the community. The Governor, who is walking ahead of his guests, meets Pearl by the window. Hester is momentarily concealed by the shadow of a curtain. Bellingham and Wilson in good humor note the child's strange beauty and insist that she is more elfin than human.

When the Governor notices Hester and realizes the relationship, his manner changes abruptly, and he immediately begins questioning Hester's ability to raise this unusual girl. Hester's first answer is calm as she says that her own sense of guilt is guarantee enough that the girl will not be taught perverse ways. But the officials are not satisfied and begin asking Pearl her catechism. The child knows the answers well enough, but with the same deliberate mischievousness that has so often tortured Hester, Pearl insists that she has not come into the world from a heavenly home; she had not been made at all, but had been plucked by her mother off the bush of wild roses that grew by the prison door. The narrator comments that this reply was probably suggested by the Governor's roses standing just outside the window.

Chillingworth, who has been standing on the edge of the group with Dimmesdale, whispers something into that man's ear. Hester is not so much fearful of what he may have said but of the great change which has come over the man; his complexion seems to have grown duskier and his figure even more misshapen than last she saw him. The Governor is shocked by the young girl's manner, and Hester, fearing that she may lose Pearl for it, turns with all of the force she can muster and insists that Dimmesdale intercede for her. He had been her pastor and knows her better than these men. Hester in a near shriek claims that he has an understanding and knowledge which the others lack; she will not lose her child and he must speak for her.

Dimmesdale comes forward with his hand on his heart, and in an excitement triggered by what he has heard, speaks on Hester's part. God gave her the child and the nature to care for it; moreover, it is the only blessing in her life and a curse for her crime. He notes that even the way the girl is dressed signifies that Hester is reminding herself of the red symbol which sears her bosom. Dimmesdale's arguments settle the matter, and he retreats to the shadow of the same curtain that had hidden Hester earlier. Pearl, in an act of affection rarely used with strangers, walks slowly to Dimmesdale and caresses his hand. As Hester and Pearl leave the mansion, they meet Mistress Hibbins, the Governor's bitter-tempered sister. She will be executed a few years later as a witch. The hag invites Hester to the woods for some real or imagined satanic rite, but Hester with a triumphal smile refuses, saying that had things gone differently she would have been of that company which signs its name in the Black Man's book.

COMMENTARY: There are many ironies in this section. The Governor lives in great pomp but still insists on the austere morality which could have furthered Hester's pain. Indeed his own sister seems a projection of his obvious double standard. When Dimmesdale exhorted Hester to confess ("The Recognition"), his remarks contained a truth which applied equally to him, and here, when Hester addresses him, her remarks have an equally forceful double meaning. Hester can insist that he speak for her because he does know more about her than anyone else: he is her partner in adultery. Hester's words, unknown to the rest of the company, carry the threat of uncovering the guilty man, and Dimmesdale is forced from his normally silent attitude to speak.

The most unusual aspect of this chapter from a technical sense is Hawthorne's uncanny ability to construct the meeting with great dramatic effect in the physical arrangements of all the characters. There are six people present during the interview, and we are always conscious of their presence, but in the way they pass in and out of the immediate action we see only the most important event at any one time. Hester is off the center of the stage as Pearl romps by the window. The Governor and Wilson come in in good spirits and joke with the youngster until they recognize her. What we are now prepared for is the grand hypocrisy of their attitude as it switches to deliberate and overworked seriousness. After Pearl's part is done and she has given the two men an excuse to be stern, Hester draws our attention as she steps into the group. When that action is over, a new dramatic relationship is started between Hester and Dimmesdale, who is at the fringe of the crowd. Then he steps forward, says his part, and then as quickly retreats into the shadows. All of this time our eyes are glimpsing Chillingworth as he whispers comments to the other members who are temporarily silent, but at no time do we suffer any distraction. It is a difficult feat to have six characters active but not intruding on a suspenseful situation, and Hawthorne is in perfect control.

IX. The Leech   Chillingworth maintains the secret of his real identity and becomes accepted into the community as a doctor, or "leech" as the term was then used. The only other surgeon did not possess much skill, and the knowledge acquired from long years of study while in Indian captivity soon gave Chillingworth a formidable reputation. Externally at least he acts the part of a thoroughly religious man at the beginning of his stay, and to foster this impression he chooses Reverend Mr. Dimmesdale as his spiritual advisor. About this same period the health of Dimmesdale begins to decline. His form grows emaciated, and his voice, though still rich and sweet, has the ring of death in it.

The people of Salem regard it as the result of too much devotion to his religious tasks. Some are not yet ready to allow such a saintly man to go to his reward; his friends insist, above all his protestations, that he confer with the new doctor, and in time the two men live together so that the man of science may be better able to care for the ailing minister. In the early part of this association, some in the community feel that Chillingworth's arrival is providential. Why else would such a learned physician find himself in this wilderness when fame and fortune were to be had in England? There can be no other reason but that he was ordained by an act of God to care for the community's most hallowed man. Chillingworth is interested in the complete person of the minister; it seems the belief of the doctor is that a man's physical ills can only be remedied by knowing all there is to know about the patient. And so Chillingworth delves deep into the patient's personality, pries into his recollections, and probes everything with such a cautious touch that one could liken him to some treasure seeker moving carefully about in a dark cave.

The house in which they live is near the cemetery. The narrator feels it is a fitting location since it reminds each man of the special problems of his calling. Science must try to overcome the too swift arrival of death, and religion prepares one for what follows. While Dimmesdale's friends regard the doctor as a gift from heaven, not all members of the community are so complacent. A few claim that the doctor resembles a man of mysterious criminal background that they had either seen or heard about in England. Some claim, too, that the Indian captivity provided knowledge of black magic, and that the seeming cures were more an indication that Chillingworth was a friend of Satan, than of God. Many of those who held varied views on the influences in the doctor's medicine and his previous history agreed that his own appearance had changed drastically since the first days of his stay. At first, his expression had been calm, meditative, and scholar-like. Now, there was something ugly and evil in his face, which they had not previously noticed and which grew still the more obvious the more often they looked at him. He seems to have been smudged with the smoke from infernal fires.

No matter what the earlier opinions, it grew to be a widely held view that Arthur Dimmesdale, like many other personages of special sanctity in all ages of the Christian world, was either haunted by Satan himself or Satan's emissary in the guise of old Roger Chillingworth. This diabolic agent had divine permission to plot against his soul, but no sensible man, it was confessed, could doubt the outcome. The minister could only come from this trial a newly-transfigured man, more saintly than ever. To judge from the gloom and terror of the minister's eyes, the battle was a difficult one and the victory anything but secure.

COMMENTARY: The unholy alliance between Dimmesdale and Chillingworth is much more than the struggle between good and evil witnessed in all ages. Ironically enough, Chillingworth illustrates the arrival of scientific detachment and methodical probing in this religiously oriented community. Chillingworth's motives are evil in intent, but the effect his methods have on the religious motives of Dimmesdale shows what happens when the easy crutch of emotionalism and superstition is put to logical analysis. This is not to say that scientific method is always correct and infallible, but rather that a slow and objective approach will uncover the fallacies of unreasonable positions. It is not science which triumphs in The Scarlet Letter but the virtue and honest religious feelings of Hester. Science, however, does help uncover the weaknesses in Dimmesdale. While Chillingworth methodically pursues the mystery in Dimmesdale's sickness, the people act with an equal degree of double-think: Dimmesdale is sick and needs curing, Chillingworth is evil but he is so evil that he cannot but help the minister to new heights of saintliness and in so doing cure the minister. It would seem that the quickest way to work a cure is to weaken the system even further by larger doses of poison until the body is forced to cure itself. Paradoxically, the community with every best intention is inflicting punishment on Dimmesdale as readily as it does on Hester for less attractive reasons.

X. The Leech and His Patient   Roger Chillingworth had begun his search, so he felt, with the objectivity and integrity of a judge. As the investigation continues, a terrible fascination grips him and his pre-occupation is now utterly morbid. While Dimmesdale realizes in a vague way that he is in the presence of some grave evil, he in no way suspects Chillingworth's probing questions or the ugly change he notices in that man's appearance. Dimmesdale in his own nature is equally morbid and suspicious of mankind, and this prevents his noticing any other source for this strange spiritual depression other than the guilt which he nourishes in his soul. The minister questions the doctor on the worth of herbs gathered from the grave of an unknown sinner. As their conversation continues, each man offers his own belief in guilt and hidden sin. For the doctor all evil should be outwardly confessed and not hidden in the tomb till judgment day. The minister insists that it is the soul's own business what it chooses to do about unacknowledged sins. While he himself has witnessed the relief that comes with the deathbed confession, he still feels that such a confession, especially from a man with a seemingly fine character, can only demoralize the society in which the sinner lives and frustrate any later act of good. The decision should be between the sinner and his God.

Just as the doctor asks which alternative is better, God's own truth or society's welfare, they see young Pearl skipping and laughing along the cemetery footpath. She dances irreverently from one grave mound to another. Hester commands her to stop and in seeming retaliation the girl gathers a handful of burrs and arranges them on her mother's dress. Sighting Dimmesdale at the window, she throws a burr at him, and he shrinks in fear. As quickly, she runs to her mother, telling her to come away before the Black Man, who has hold of the minister, gets Hester in his grasp as well.

As the men pursue their conversation, the doctor notes that Dimmesdale's sickness is a reflection of his soul's condition; only if he knows the character of the minister's spiritual ailment can he effect a cure. With a frantic gesture Dimmesdale rushes from the room, and now the doctor is more sure than ever that he is close to some important discovery. After a few hours alone, the minister returns to speak to the doctor. All seems forgotten. Not long after this interview, while Dimmesdale is in an unusually deep sleep, the doctor walks quietly into the minister's study and stealthily uncovers the sleeping man's chest. What he sees or imagines he sees there sends Chillingworth into a satanic rapture. Every feature is distorted in obscene pleasure as he throws his arms over his head and stomps his feet on the floor.

COMMENTARY:　　Like all the important conversations so far, the talk between the doctor and his patient contains a double truth; each man offers a logical possibility for a position taken, but each is also excusing his present conduct. The doctor's character has already been painted with unattractive traits, and the beginning paragraph is only a summary of his evil progress. However, for the first time Dimmesdale's conversation shows that he is not only a moral coward, but a hypocrite as well. The succeeding chapter only confirms this impression. One wonders what Hester saw in the parson in the first place. While the doctor's manner in his alleged discovery and his purpose seem devoid of any goodness, what he has said about the effects of guilt have been borne out by the mental sciences. A man's disposition affects his physical being as thoroughly as any poison or medicine can. It is a great irony that the misshapen man of science utters the truth to a religious man too blind to see it at work even in the man acting as his doctor. At the root of Dimmesdale's ignorance is his unrelieved pessimism. He undervalues himself and others so utterly that he can hardly distinguish good and evil.

It is important to realize that the narrator never says here what the doctor saw or thought he saw. If we are carried away by his horrible grimmacing, we will see only a scarlet letter on the minister's chest. In effect we would then be operating under the same bias that controls the doctor's life. Then the narrator can insist that we are as prone to evil as any Salem citizen. Indeed this may have been the reason for the manner of this closing paragraph. What has been described is *only* the doctor's reaction, and that reaction is ordained by his morbid purposes; it is not necessarily triggered by any real scarlet image. As Chillingworth reacts, so he is.

There are two dancing figures for contrast here. Pearl jumps from mound to mound, mocking death and the pessimism she senses in Dimmesdale, Chillingworth, and the scarlet letter on Hester. While her actions are entirely reasonable, the over-burdened adults make it impossible to avoid the symbolic quality of her action. However, Pearl the laughing young girl is only teasing her mother. The remarks she makes about Dimmesdale and his physician are only the whispering gossip she has over-heard from adults. She throws the burr at Dimmesdale not because she senses (as we would like to feel) that he is her hidden father, but because she rejects all persons in authority who have isolated her mother. Dimmesdale and Chillingworth note as she goes by that she has spattered water on the Governor only a few days previous. Pearl in her merriment is only protecting Hester.

Roger Chillingworth also dances, but his posture is the contrary of Pearl's. His joy is nearly complete because he is at last able to torment his patient to the fullest. His dance is not a mockery of death or pessimism; it is a perversely gleeful salute to the worst in man—in himself and in Dimmesdale. In effect he is dancing to celebrate the death of the heart. And when we re-member the joy of a dancing Pearl earlier, we realize how far from youth and how close to decay he is.

XI. The Interior of a Heart   No longer is the physician a spectator; now he is a chief actor in the minister's interior world. And although Dimmesdale is aware of some evil presence, because of his own depressive nature he suspects no one. Instead he chides himself for being uncomfortable in Chillingworth's company and tries to be even more cordial than necessary. Dimmesdale's decay only furthers his saintly reputation. The congregation feels that their minister speaks not only from the heart but through heavenly experiences. In their eyes the very ground on which he walks is sanctified.

Dimmesdale, on the other hand, wonders if grass can ever grow over his grave, so foul is his conscience. In his tor-ments Dimmesdale has the half-formed desire to confess; his sermons stress the ignominy of his nature. But as often as he tells them that his life is a pollution and a lie, so often does his congregation revere him the more. He knows that his public confessions are not specific enough to suggest the truth, but he continues the breast-beating which seems as much hypocrisy as it is more self-inflicted torture for the hidden sin. There are private reprisals as well. He scourges himself bloody and fasts and keeps long vigils before his mirror. The constant introspection does not purify: On one of these ugly nights, after visions and illusions of spec-ters reeling in his mirror, he dresses in his ministerial robes and quietly leaves the house.

COMMENTARY: Another weakness is added to the character of Dimmes-
                     dale; not only is he a coward, he is also a spiritual
masochist. The ghostly parade before his mirror is reminiscent of
Hester's time on the scaffold, only hers was for the most part a
relief from woe. By now the ambivalent remarks of our character
should be a familiar device: the sermons not only carry a double
meaning: one for Dimmesdale, another for the congregation, but
they also have a double purpose, for Dimmesdale is not only trying in a half-hearted fashion to ease his conscience in the adultery,
he is also trying to punish himself for the hypocrisy which triggers
the sermons in the first place.

XII. The Minister's Vigil   Dimmesdale walks to the scaffold. It has been
                              seven years since Hester stood there, but the
memory is as if it were yesterday. It is a cloudy night in early May, and
the town sleeps quietly. As he stands there, Dimmesdale feels that the
act is much like his other public confessions and secret penances. Since
there is little chance of discovery, Dimmesdale cries aloud and momem-
tarily feels he will be finally discovered, but the cry is no more than a
whimper. Only Governor Bellingham, who sleeps lightly, and his sister
Mistress Hibbins have heard the noise, but they soon return to bed.

                    Dimmesdale becomes comparatively calm
again, and he notices a lantern light approaching in the darkness. It is
Reverend Wilson returning from the death-bed of former Governor Winthrop. As Wilson passes, Dimmesdale imagines that he speaks out inviting
the old man up there with him. This illusion is followed by a series of
hallucinations. Now Dimmesdale sees the village gradually awake and
all rushing to gape at the forlorn figure. Carried away by the grotesque
horror of this picture, he begins laughing, and it is only the sight of Pearl
and Hester returning from the same death-bed that restores his sense of
reality.

                    The invitation he utters now is heard, and the
three join hands on the platform. Dimmesdale, for the first time since
Hester's trial, feels new life rushing through him as he touches Pearl and
Hester. Pearl seems moved by the seriousness of the occasion, and she asks
if he will join hands again at tomorrow noon, but the minister gives
only half an answer: they will all join hands on judgment day. Pearl
laughs. Before Dimmesdale finishes his explanation a meteor lights the
sky, and the three stand illumined: Hester with her scarlet letter,
Dimmesdale with his hand on his heart, and Pearl as the link between
the two adults. Pearl now seems touched with witchcraft in the strange
light, and she points to Roger Chillingworth standing near the scaffold.
Dimmesdale is terrified of the weird appearance of the man, and he bends
to hear what Pearl has to say about him. The child mumbles gibberish

in his ear and laughs again. She scolds him for his cowardice, and a shaken minister is led home by the doctor. The day following is Sunday, and Dimmesdale delivers his most powerful sermon to date.

COMMENTARY: Dimmesdale's early reactions on the scaffold show how close to insanity he is. This is the second of three scaffold scenes, and it indicates that the action will rush downwards now to its inevitable conclusion. While the three people seem a tableau representing the happy Christian family, their presence on the scaffold is tainted with Dimmesdale's fear. If anything, the three are a mockery of family life and of the love which exists between Hester and Pearl *because* of Dimmesdale. Chillingworth does not feel this, of course; the company before him with its supposed unity will only give him more cause for spite as he thinks of the family life he has been denied.

Pearl is only a child and there is no reason to suppose that she is aware of the special significance of this meeting. She has asked for a friend and protector who will publicly associate himself with her and her equally outcast mother. She is denied and she chides Dimmesdale, because she is too young to be satisfied with abstractions about judgment day. When he bends to hear what she has to say about the doctor, she is only teasing a man who has been, she feels, a tease himself.

Our own interpretative minds will not leave the meanings on this level. Dimmesdale holds the key to his salvation, and action, not abstraction, will save him. He cannot understand Pearl's mutterings because he cannot understand himself; he has been denied any special insight into the role of Chillingworth because he has refused to do anything positive to earn that insight. Pearl is the link between Hester and the minister; she is here not an elfin sprite but truth and honest action, and Dimmesdale does not have the courage to clasp it with both hands.

XIII. Another View of Hester

Hester finally notices how badly the doctor's association has affected Dimmesdale. Strangely enough, as Dimmesdale has become progressively weaker, Hester has become more perceptive and resilient in the face of adversity. Since she no longer fought the public's somber sympathies, it has come to accept her. The "A" has come to mean "Able" — for all the occasions she has so ably comforted the down-trodden. The letter has the effect of the cross on a nun's bosom. In fact, it is believed by many that an Indian had drawn his arrow against the badge, and that the missile struck it but fell harmless to the ground.

Hester is nun-like in other ways as well, for her outward appearance is no longer marked with the luxuriant beauty of former days. Her hair is now hidden under her cap, and there is no external evidence of any romantic, feminine tenderness. While all such qualities have been crushed deeply into her heart, the power of her intellect has grown. Because she has been deprived of all social communion, she has recourse to much speculation. Had the religious leaders realized how far ranging were her thoughts, they would have held it a deadlier crime than that stigmatized by the scarlet letter. Indeed, had little Pearl never come into her life, she might have come down in history as the foundress of a religious sect. She thinks long and hard upon the position of women in society and eventually concludes that society must be torn down and reshaped if woman is ever to take her rightful place next to man. Women themselves will have to be re-educated in the same process. Now, however, her night-meeting with Dimmesdale has given her a new theme for reflection. She sees that he is on the verge of lunacy and questions the wisdom of her pact with her husband. Not long after having resolved to meet Chillingworth, she meets the old man at the sea side as he looks for roots and herbs for his medicines.

COMMENTARY: Hester's gradual rise to a new power demonstrates that the doctor's earlier conversation with Dimmesdale to the effect that honesty is the best policy is true. However pleasing this may seem, one cannot forget the terrible sacrifice Hester has made for her present intellectual insights. In the manner in which her state of mind is described, it is easy to see that Hester has become as cool and objective in her analysis as Chillingworth is calculating in his pursuit of the parson. It is possible to construct a spectrum of mental states and attitudes at this point: Dimmesdale and his congregation can represent various sorts of religious belief unbuttressed with any reasonableness; Chillingworth has an equal amount of fervor but it is applied to revenge through a scientific (psychological) medium; Hester still crushed by a heritage of guilt is at least detached enough to think coolly of life's problems and at the same time believe in God, and Pearl can represent man fully confident of his own individuality and powers of reason under a benevolent God.

Although young Pearl's development has not been presented in great detail, we know that she is an intelligent and sensitive child. One must not forget that, although she is unique because of her mother's sin and the suggestion of various supernatural influences, her greatest character former is her mother. And with her childish intellect she is imbibing the same freedom of speculation as her mother. She acts originally and unconventionally because her mother has become original and unconventional in her new life of thought. Socially Pearl could never be accepted because of her mother's history, but more importantly, she could never accept this Salem society because it is morally and intellectually foreign to her.

XIV. Hester and the Physician   Pearl plays with the shells and seaweed as her mother talks to the physician. She flits like a bird from one shore pool to another watching her broken reflection in the water. The doctor's manner seems almost pleasant, and he commends Hester on her growing reputation of good deeds in the community. He mentions that the elders had even said that the "A" might be removed and he himself had praised the idea; but Hester insists that if it is God's wish, it will fall off without the council of the magistrates.

Hester's attention is not on herself but on the appearances wrought in these seven years on Chillingworth. His face seems lit by the same infernal flame many felt glowed in years past on Hester's letter. Roger Chillingworth is a striking evidence of man's faculty for transforming himself into a devil. Still conscious of her role in all of this, she feels that she is in some part responsible for Chillingworth's ruin. As Hester begins asking that the doctor cease this course of revenge, the man gloats on the pitiable condition of Dimmesdale. He insists further that it is not in his power to stop or to forgive. He laments Hester's suffering in part and says that he is aware that she has an uncommon character and should have had the good fortune to meet a better man than he before their marriage. Hester may do what she wishes, but it is all too late; they can only allow suffering and evil to flourish as it will.

COMMENTARY: It is difficult to decide where truth stops and spiteful cunning begins in the doctor's remarks. In all that he says we are conscious of the well-meaning man that was once there nine years ago, but we should also realize that his manner is still dictated by his present aim—the anguish of Dimmesdale. If there is one new and striking revelation in Chillingworth's statements it is the fatalism of his closing sentence. He, of course, may be excusing himself when insisting that all is outside his control, but he is repeating the same dark philosophy we have heard from Dimmesdale and seen in his attitude toward his fellow man. It is another way of demonstrating that each man controls his own destiny; Dimmesdale, though tormented by Chillingworth's machinations, is nonetheless being punished by his own outlook. The doctor is only the external manifestation of this dreadful pessimism, and when Dimmesdale dies, so will the doctor.

XV. Hester and Pearl   Roger Chillingworth goes his way stooping along
the ground in search of his medicines. Hester won-
ders if the earth will be scorched by his passing, so evil seems his manner
and his soul. The longer she thinks about the man the more vehement she
becomes, until every memory of their life together is hateful. For the first
time she feels that he has done more harm to her than she ever did to
him. Pearl, who has been busy playing all the while, has become bored
with the shore's sea trinkets, and she makes the letter A in seaweed on
her bosom. She wonders at its meaning, realizing somehow that it contains more than just a sound, or the shape she has learned from her horn-
book (the alphabetical table used to teach spelling).

When her mother asks her why she wears the
green letter, Pearl answers that it is for the same reason that the minister
keeps his hand over his heart. Hester sees the answer as incongruous and
questions Pearl further, but the child insists that is all she knows. In the
way in which Pearl answers and because of the serious and guileless expression on her face, Hester senses that the child is attempting to express
some grave confidence, but there is no other explanation forthcoming.
Several times that day and on the morning following, Pearl asks the
meaning of the letter and the reason for Dimmesdale's hand on his heart.
Hester is upset by the teasing and threatens to put Pearl in the closet for
punishment unless she stops.

COMMENTARY: This chapter acts as a transition. We have been told of
the condition of each character, and the new Hester has
finally matured. She is no longer terrified of Chillingworth, and
although Pearl's questions are not pleasant in effect, they no longer
move Hester to pangs of remorse. Pearl's question is important:
what does the letter mean? For Hester the fiery and painful suffering of the stigma has been eased—or better, transferred to Dimmesdale; she may as well be wearing the cool green letter of seaweed
formed by Pearl.

XVI. A Forest Walk   Hester remains determined to tell Dimmesdale the
truth about Chillingworth. Several days later she
finds out that the minister has gone into the forest to talk to an Indian
missionary, and she sets out to meet him on his return. The day is chilly
and somber, and the cloudy sky allows only momentary gleams of sunshine which seem to deliberately retreat before Hester. Not so with Pearl,
if anything the girl seems to draw whatever sun there is to where she is
standing. Only as Hester approaches Pearl does the sunlight vanish and
appear elsewhere.

Hester rests from her walk, and Pearl demands a story, not any story but one about the Black Man who haunts the forest. Pearl says that he carries a heavy black book listing the names of those who meet him here among the trees. Hester wonders at the source of this tale, and Pearl tells that it was an old woman at the house they had ministered in the previous night. The crone had said that Mistress Hibbins' name was in the book and that Hester's scarlet letter was his mark as well. In return for no more questions Hester admits that once she did meet this Black Man and that the letter was his mark. The forest grows thicker, but in the midst of the great trees and the maze of underbrush they discover a small stream as melancholy sounding as the forest atmosphere itself. After a few childish questions about its source and sounds, Pearl begins playing at its wandering margin. At the same time Hester hears someone walking nearby.

COMMENTARY: Pearl's incessant questioning is indicative of her evergrowing intellectual awareness. As mentioned earlier, she is her mother's child insofar as she reflects (in a childish fashion) a pensive concern for life's incongruities and injustices. Light and water are continually associated with young Pearl; this is the author's way of demonstrating how unusual her nature is. Hester, though intellectually free, cannot capture sunshine, because her vivacity is gone, but young Pearl can and does on every occasion. The gossip about the Black Man is also a way of fostering the diabolical nature of Chillingworth and the pessimism of Dimmesdale. In previous chapters young Pearl has referred to both men as "the Black Man." When Hester mentions her meeting with the "Black Man" she is merely trying to end an uncomfortable line of questions and, in a cryptic way, acknowledge her guilt. However, one cannot help but think of the two "Black Men" who have caused her so much sorrow.

XVII. The Pastor and His Parishioner   Hester and Dimmesdale greet each other in the dark wood like two wandering spirits. Instinctively they both walk deeper into the shadows and silently brood upon the past. After some meaningless remarks about the overcast weather, each asks if the other has found any peace. Hester looks down at the scarlet letter, and the minister begins speaking of his ever-increasing life of despair. The growing reputation of saintliness has made it all the more impossible to live in any hope of tranquility. Hester's urgings that he *has* repented only increase the present state of his despair. Hester tells him of Chillingworth's secret and apologizes for keeping this from him. For one brief moment after his initial disbelief, the minister's face is covered with the same dark frown seen on the doctor's visage. After an impassioned plea for her forgiveness, the minister excuses Hester. They are not the worst sinners after all, for Chillingworth had done more than they; he has violated the sanctity of the human heart in cold blood.

The weather grows more forbidding, and the minister begins asking Hester for more advice. He is worried that the doctor will now reveal their secret, and Hester talks of escaping to London. He despairs again because he knows he cannot survive anywhere alone especially if it means deserting his vocation. Hester answers that she will go with him wherever he wishes to lead a new life in God's service.

COMMENTARY: Hester is the activist here. Dimmesdale has been given all the facts of his situation, but he is powerless. Even before seeing what happens in the following chapters, one should realize that this pact is impossible. Hester is only comforting another dying member of the Salem community, but she does not yet realize it.

XVIII. A Flood of Sunshine   Dimmesdale gazes into Hester's face with a look of joy and hope; but it is not purely this, for fear shines there as well and a horror at her boldness. He cannot appreciate the native courage of her mind because his own mind had been broken down by long and exquisite suffering. However, her fortitude and the promise of her companionship revive this fallen spirit, and he feels as though he has been born again. To complete their pact for a new life together, Hester throws her scarlet letter on the ground near the stream. With the stigma gone, Hester sighs with relief as the burden of shame lifts from her. Her cheeks glow with a new freshness, and, as if heaven smiles on all this, sunshine pours into the forest.

All seems radiant now, and they begin talking of Pearl and how she will react. Dimmesdale confesses that he is uncomfortable in the presence of all children and with Pearl especially. The girl is playing some distance from the couple, and the quivering light changes her appearance from child to apparition and back again. Pearl's time in the wood has not been spent with such anxiety. Nature seemed to be her companion: forest animals greet her on her way, and wildflowers seem to beg her to decorate her gay-colored clothing even more. Hester calls the child, and she moves in her magical fashion towards them. She moves slowly now, for she has seen the clergyman.

COMMENTARY: The narrator in this last chapter has done much to bolster our expectations for an idyllic future for Hester and Dimmesdale. Nature smiles and a darkened wood is now blessed with sunshine. Even Pearl's appearance corroborates the benign atmosphere. But this scene is not over; the scarlet letter has not been washed away by the stream. It lies at the water's edge.

XIX. The Child at the Brookside.   Hester continues to reassure Dimmesdale that Pearl and he will have no trouble getting along. The minister seems to have his mind on other concerns as he mentions his fears that others might notice Pearl's partial resemblance to him. As Pearl approaches, Hester, as if to prepare Dimmesdale for an unusual behavior on Pearl's part, talks of how unconventional the child has been at times, and this only furthers the minister's anxiety as he again notes his own awkwardness with children. By this time Pearl, bedecked with flowers, has reached the edge of the brook, and she gazes silently at Hester and Dimmesdale seated together on a mossy tree trunk. Where she has stopped, the brook is so mirrorlike in its smoothness that it has the effect of changing the appearance of the girl. She seems as one returning from another world seeking a more tangible self in the company of her mother. Even the minister notes that the brook seems the boundary between two worlds, and he encourages Hester to hurry Pearl across. Hester asks as much, but the child is silent.

Pearl searches the faces of the two before her, and, as she points to her mother's bosom, a frown clouds her face. In the next instant she is screaming and gesturing in a fit of anger. Hester, trying to remain calm, suggests to a shaken Dimmesdale that a child will abide no change in a parent's dress or behavior: Pearl misses the scarlet letter. Hester's placating words work to no avail, and she retrieves the letter and places it again on her dress. Pearl then admits to knowing her mother and jumps across the stream. But the clergyman is yet to be approached, and Pearl, who recalls his refusal on the scaffold is more than reluctant to talk to him. When he gingerly kisses her on the forehead, she rushes to the stream and washes the kissed spot, and further refuses to join her mother's company until the time they leave for home.

COMMENTARY: This chapter contains the finest handling of Pearl's seemingly double nature. Hester (and the narrator) has given us every natural reason for her rejecting Dimmesdale and Hester's new appearance; the child is jealous of a rival and suspicious of of this unusual change in her mother. However, Pearl's natural reactions seem to counter Hester's present happiness and future joy nonetheless, and one wonders if Hawthorne has shown Pearl here as spiteful and satanic as Chillingworth is. Pearl as elfin or angelic spirit is indeed uncomfortable now in the presence of Dimmesdale, but not because of any maliciousness, rather by her very constitution she cannot abide the pessimistic character of the man. If there is any place in the novel where the full character of Pearl's free spirit is shown and used, it is here. In short, the actions of Pearl the human and Pearl the elfin angel are quite consistent. It is obvious that Dimmesdale is far too weak to ever handle familial responsibility just as he is far too somber to do anything but destroy Hester's present confidence in herself and the love that exists between Hester and Pearl. Pearl, as the elfin spirit, sees only the death of Hester's present self in this contract with Dimmesdale, hence the mad screaming. It is better that Hester carry the symbol of guilt on her dress than have her carry the weighted and ruined soul of Dimmesdale. What would then happen to the intellectual freedom she has won?

If there is sadness in this chapter, it is that Hester is not fully aware of how much she has changed from her former passionate and vivacious self. It is touching to see that even the "new" Hester desires some of the personality of the old, and we are again reminded of how much that transformation cost. But we should not lament Hester's return to the scarlet letter. That decision had been made seven years ago.

The chapter also shows the fallibility of Hester. In our admiration of her new strength we should not forget she is flesh and blood. Her present misguided attraction to Dimmesdale is reminiscent of the former unthinking, emotional attraction that existed between these two. She in some ways is a better and nobler person, but she is, as she was then, a lonely woman, starved for the companionship of an adult. She has not transcended her guilt and suffering; rather, they have transformed her.

XX. The Minister in a Maze   Dimmesdale and Hester separate, still feeling that they can count on a new life together despite the present feelings of Pearl, and Hester has said that she will make arrangements to sail for Bristol on a newly-arrived ship in Salem harbor. While Hester's outlook has been somewhat darkened by the return of the letter, Dimmesdale suffers from a strange new vitality. There is no suggestion of joy in all of this, rather it is an excitement touched with an unusual confidence—almost as if he were sharing some secret joke. The town in his eyes seems to exist in a different light; all is as it was, but heightened by another coloration.

Before he reaches home, there are other evidences of a revolution in his thought and feeling—indeed in his entire moral code. When he meets one of the older deacons, Dimmesdale can hardly refrain from uttering some blasphemous suggestion. Again, meeting a widow of many years who had sustained herself with Scripture and the pleasant converse of Dimmesdale, the minister is so moved to some disparaging remark on the immortality of the soul that he could hardly make himself intelligible. What he did say, he could never remember, but it was so unclear that it had that same effect as some soothing moralism. Dimmesdale is so indifferent to the greeting of a young girl of the congregation that she feels she is the guilty party and spends a tear-filled day brooding over the cause of her fault. Only one person, Mistress Hibbins, seems to notice the apparent satanic change in his nature, and she accuses him in a confident manner of having made a pact with the devil on his forest walk.

This last meeting shakes him somewhat, and he becomes suspicious of his hope, wondering if it has any virtue. Mistress Hibbins has only reminded him of his essentially pessimistic nature. Nonetheless, in his meeting at home with Chillingworth he has enough confidence to deny any further need for his medicines; the fresh air, he claims, and nature's pleasant influence have fortified his health. Through the manner of Dimmesdale's remarks, the doctor knows he is no longer a trusted associate. Dimmesdale eats a hearty meal and begins anew the Election Sermon he is to deliver the day before the ship leaves. He works through the night with such ecstasy that he wonders how such a befouled soul can be the vehicle for such inspiration.

COMMENTARY: The manner of Dimmesdale's return to town shows that Hester's ministerings have not changed him. He cannot allow himself joy, and his secret thoughts about the people he meets show that he is no more removed from mental and spiritual disintegration than he was that night on the scaffold. He is little more than a cluster of silly and childish fancies. Even in his supposedly good humor, he tempts himself to various actions he has not the courage to carry out. When he discovers that the boat leaves the day after his sermon, he confesses that he is glad. However, he does not specify all the reasons for being pleased; he merely says that he can leave with the impression that he has performed his church duties to the last. This shows that he is in part still concerned with his reputation. What Dimmesdale does not yet know, but what we should remember, is that many people will feel he has maintained himself in virtue to the last: it is on Election Day that he will confess his guilt in spite of himself, and in spite of his good intentions in this act, he will leave a holy reputation behind. Courageless, Dimmesdale will die as he lived—fostering hypocrisy.

XXI. The New England Holiday   This is the day the new Governor is to
                                     receive his office, and Salem is bustling
with activity. The narrator shows a touch of cynicism as he comments
that, while much of this might seem funereal for a visitor, the citizenry
was allowing itself as much excitement as possible under the circumstances. Pearl talks to Hester about the strange behavior of the minister; in
the daylight he does not recognize them, but in the darkness of the forest and on the scaffold at night he speaks to them. Hester hushes the
girl and tells her to fix her attention on the advancing procession and
milling crowd. Not only is all of Salem present but also rough-looking
seamen from the ship.

                                     Roger Chillingworth enters the market
place in the company of the ship's captain. After some conversation, the
gaily-decorated captain, whose garb seems even more exotic than Pearl's
leaves the doctor and passes through the crowd. When he and Hester
meet, it is not long before she discovers that Chillingworth has booked
passage on the same ship. He claims to be in trouble with the religious
authorities.

  COMMENTARY: In a manner similar to the opening chapters the stage
                     has again been set for some revelation. Dimmesdale is
again in the company of the hierarchy, and Chillingworth stands
on the edge of the crowd milling in the market place. However,
there is only one revelation possible, for Hester's sin has already
been exposed.

XXII. The Procession   Hester can hardly pull her thoughts about Chil-
                             lingworth's actions together when the procession
makes its way into the market place. Dimmesdale walks behind the
eminent civil authorities with new energy and exuberance. Yet if the
clergyman were rightly viewed, his strength seemed not of the body, and
so abstracted was his look that it was unlikely he heard the processional
music. On gazing at Dimmesdale walking proudly past wrapped in all
the majesty of his office, Hester realizes that they exist in separate worlds.
In despair and disappointment Hester thinks it unfair of Dimmesdale to
be able to withdraw himself so completely from the world they had
created in the forest. Pearl responds to her mother's mood and asks if
this is the same minister who kissed her in the wood. If it is in fact the
same man, Pearl says she will willingly kiss him now in the daylight.

                             Mistress Hibbins has noticed the minister, and in
her eccentric fashion she begins speaking of Hester's and Dimmesdale's
meeting in the woods. Hester denies it all, but with the amount of information Hibbins has, it is probable that she had seen (but not overheard)

the two together on one of her frequent and mysterious trips to the forest. She continues by saying that Dimmesdale's secret pact with the devil will someday be revealed in public just as Hester's sin was. With a shrill laugh the weird woman takes her leave.

By this time in the church the preliminary prayer has been offered, and Dimmesdale's voice peals through the crowd in all its melancholy richness. Hester stands outside at the foot of the scaffold listening as if the sermon was meant for her ears alone. Pearl is not interested, and she wanders away from the crowd only to meet the captain. He is bewitched by the youngster and tries to kiss her. In his fondness he grabs only at the air, for Pearl is as quick as a hummingbird. He does give her a gold chain and a fateful message to carry to her mother: Chillingworth has said that he will escort Dimmesdale to the ship personally. This information is not the only reason for Hester's confusion; the Salem citizens excited anew by the curiosity of the visitors over Hester's letter and its reputation have gathered with the others in a circle about her. Hester recognizes the same matrons in the crowd who gossiped and jeered on that earlier day. It would seem that just as she is about to begin a new life and throw her letter aside, it blazes again in torturing shame. Dimmesdale looks down on all from his pulpit.

COMMENTARY: Most all of the *dramatis personae* should be so clearly understood in their motivation by now that there is no major problem of interpretation. If Hawthorne's literary style has any flaw, it is that he continually repeats and redefines actions or symbols associated with characters, and in so doing takes the chance of lessening our own imaginative participation at those places. However, even in this criticism one must keep in mind the discursive manner of much nineteenth-century fiction, that is to say, discursive by our standards. Life, and that includes fictional life, was slower in tempo, and readers were prepared to spend time listening to repeated themes.

The presence of Mistress Hibbins may seem one of these unneeded repetitions. Earlier she is a convenient figure to underscore the hypocrisy and superstition that exists in the mansions of the mighty. However, one may feel that her talk with Hester is superfluous to the present action. Chillingworth is still an ever-hovering and in no way diminished threat, and we know that no one would listen to Hibbins even if she did talk before Dimmesdale confesses. Then why have her repeat what we have already seen? The one satisfactory answer is that she exists not so much for the action as for the atmosphere. Dimmesdale is lost in his sermon, Chillingworth is in the background plotting, and Hester is lost in the confusion of her own doubts and the hubbub of the crowd. Hibbins' momentary presence not only locates Hester among all the people, but she also prepares us for the confusion and horror to happen shortly. Hawthorne wants to remind us again that anguish, fear, spite, and the like are not abstractions or mere states of mind; they are things as real as the eccentric Hibbins, and they walk abroad embodied and embodying people.

XXIII. The Revelation of the Scarlet Letter

Dimmesdale's tremulous voice has reached every corner of the church, and the congregation stands spellbound as he speaks of the new civilization being cut out of the New England wilderness and the new destiny for these newly gathered people of the Lord. As the parishioners reach the open area of the market place, their rapture breaks into speech. According to their united testimony, never had any man spoken in so wise, so high, and so holy a spirit as he had this day. But through it all there has been a certain deep, sad undertone of pathos which could not be interpreted other than as the natural regret of one soon to die. This sense of his transitory stay on earth gave the final emphasis to the effect felt by all, that the preacher was an inspired angel who had shaken his bright wings over the Salem people and showered golden truths upon them. He stands, at this moment, on the very pinnacle of his spiritual reputation and his eloquence. Hester still stands beside the scaffold of the pillory.

Once again the procession of magistrates moves through the crowd which in highly charged spirit shouts its acclaim for the venerated preacher. As Dimmesdale moves through the crowd, its cries fall into murmurs; his disposition is drastically changed, as if all the eloquence had drained his life's blood. Reverend Wilson steps forward to offer his arm, but the young minister waves him back. As Dimmesdale reaches Pearl and Hester, he pauses, and before Governor Bellingham can reach him to offer assistance to the awaiting festivities, Dimmesdale stretches his arms towards the scaffold and calls Pearl and Hester to his side. Chillingworth is nearby; rushing through the mass of surprised people, he shouts at Dimmesdale to stop this madness. Chillingworth claims he can still save him from death and that there is no need to die in dishonor. Dimmesdale shouts back at his tempter, and again he calls to Hester and the girl and asks the woman's help up the stairs. Roger Chillingworth follows the company up the stairs and amidst the tumult reviles the minister with further torments.

Supported by Hester and holding Pearl's hand, Dimmesdale faces the magistrates and begins his confession in a glaring sunlight which seems to separate his figure from the others standing there with him. As Dimmesdale finishes, he tears open his clothing as if to show some hideous and hidden wound to the terror-stricken multitude. As he collapses, Chillingworth bends over Dimmesdale and cries that he has escaped him. In all this the doctor's appearance has changed also, and he seems to be as bloodless as his one-time victim. There is not much time, and young Pearl gives all her childish and tear-filled love to this man in a single kiss. Hester asks if they shall at least be together in the life hereafter, but Dimmesdale still has too much remorse to comfort her even now, and he dies reminding her of their sin and the ever-present justice of God.

COMMENTARY: In the last of the three scaffold scenes, all the major characters have been finally brought together. The various characters need no verbal amplification to show all of their relationships one to the other, and Hawthorne gives us very little editorializing in the action. Here again Hawthorne has constructed a tableau. For us at least it is clear that it is a perfect picture of all the anguish in the love triangle. Hawthorne has re-employed several of the actions or images associated earlier with certain characters to solidify the final role of all here present. Hester stands by as an angel of mercy buttressing the weak and ministering to the dying. The doctor bends over the dying man as a real physician would to administer the last physical comforts. Only here he only tries to pour more poison into the man soon to be a corpse.

Dimmesdale for the first time is bathed in the full light so often associated with Pearl, and yet his confession is tinctured with the hypocrisy and cowardly masochism we have noted earlier. His speech begins with "I" but ends in the third person. He rips open his clothing to inflict as much punishment as possible on himself at this last minute, but it is done in such apparent anguish that part of the crowd at least (as we read in the next chapter) is not entirely sure of his reason or his explanation. And, of course, his final words show that he is still committed to a pessimistic view of himself *and* Hester. He cannot comfort Hester, he merely says, "His (God's) will be done." Dimmesdale can claim only to have ransomed himself from hell-fire by his final "triumphant agony" (his words), but he is in no way convinced that his love for Hester and hers for him is worth anything. The question then arises whether Dimmesdale dies in this fashion to exonerate Hester or to free himself from more torment here and hereafter? There is no final answer because Hawthorne has kept the workings of Dimmesdale's mind this last day hidden from us. But we know certainly that Dimmesdale died as pessimistically as he lived.

Pearl is not unaffected by what has happened. The narrator tells us that she cries in sympathy for the first time in her life, and that as she kissed her father, she became a complete human being enabled now to grow within the joys and sorrows of any ordinary life. What we are being told, of course, is that Pearl need no longer be regarded as the elfin angelic creature of previous times. Her role as reminder of hypocrisy is no longer needed. This may seem like so much allegorical magic on Hawthorne's part, i.e., since the spirit of evil and hypocrisy has been vanquished, Pearl's supernatural character is no longer needed as a foil. However, any tremendous emotional experience can change the alienated personality of a youngster to a more conventional and social outlook, and this is precisely what Pearl has had happen to her here. She has briefly won a father, learned to love someone besides her mother, and gained an ally from the society which estranged her, and she is the better for this. On the symbolic level a similar change must happen, and it does; but one is not necessarily a supernatural consequence of the other, rather the symbolic change is a literary consequence of a change in Pearl's natural personality and environment.

Chillingworth's position in all this tumult is never clearer than these final minutes. Hawthorne gives us nothing to remind us of the man Chillingworth, instead we see the figure of Satan hovering over a departing soul. Pearl is fully human now and Hester always was, but the physician is a caricature from some medieval representation of the fallen angel. Gerard Manley Hopkins wrote something about the essence of man and all natural objects which applies especially to Chillingworth: "What I do is me, for that I came." Chillingworth has become the sum total of the unnatural things he has done.

XXIV. Conclusion   Most people in the crowd testify to having seen a scarlet letter on the minister's exposed chest, but the reasons for it are variously interpreted. Some feel that Dimmesdale actually branded himself with the letter; others think that the doctor produced it with his satanic medicines; and another group believes that remorse, reflecting Heaven's displeasure, inflicted the stigma from within until it seared through to the surface. The narrator cannot say which of these theories is accurate, and he confesses only to bringing all opinions for the reader's judgment. There were some highly respectable witnesses who claimed never to have seen any such mark; these further claimed that nothing in the minister's remarks affirmed any conclusive association with Hester and her sin; what the minister was trying to do was, as he had always done, debase his own virtue out of his overpowering humility.

Within the year of the death of the minister, Chillingworth passed away. Two men so closely linked could not exist singularly. In his death Chillingworth left a considerable fortune to Pearl, and she became the richest heiress of her day. But the money was not to be shared in any marriage to a Salem Puritan, and soon after the doctor's death, Hester and the child left for England, where Pearl eventually married into some aristocratic family. Hester, however, returned to Salem, where her life had its only meaning. Her reputation had grown large during the years of her travel and the days remaining to her were spent in nothing but honorable regard on the part of her neighbors. She was now fully the angel of mercy with no suggestion of stigma attached to the scarlet letter still fixed to her dress. Letters from Pearl brought some joy into her life, but the character of the woman was, nonetheless, permanently fixed in sadness. After a long life of ministering hope and comfort to the sick, Hester is buried near the sunken grave of Dimmesdale. On the simple state tombstone is marked the letter "A" touched by a strange and gloomy light.

COMMENTARY: The conclusion reflects the pervasive pessimism of our narrator and his subject. The confusion over the causes and alleged appearance of the scarlet letter affirms the point made often in the story that evil or beauty is in the eye of the beholder. It is not necessary that anything miraculous happened in this tale, although it may have; what is important is what people believed happened. The "highly respectable" witnesses are first declaring their fixed attitude towards Hester and Dimmesdale; if we wish, we may take their opinion as a valid estimation, but we need not. Hawthorne, in presenting this part of popular opinion and the others, is re-establishing the objectivity he claimed in "The Custom House." As was noted in the earlier sections, Pearl and Hester cannot be other than what their view of life makes them. Hester cannot recapture what she began losing in the pact with Chillingworth, and sad and unnatural as it may be, mother and child could never exist in the same atmosphere. Hester dies with the sadness of her life, but not in despair. In being buried next to Dimmesdale, she shows still the hope for love she always had in varying degrees for this man. Her choice seems a misguided one when we consider all that Dimmesdale did and failed to do for her, but love is a mystery at best.

CRITICAL ANALYSIS

If there is a sensibility that colors the entire work and each of its characters it is that of shame. Each one of the principals is in some way
touched by it. Pearl's personality is mitigated by the shameful actions of
a spiteful community and by the shamefilled nature of her mother. Like
most children, Pearl has an innocent intensity and playfulness in that
intensity. Being as strong-willed as her mother once was, her only reaction to the sorrow she sees around her is to try to adopt it to her own
ends. This is why she plays with Hester in what seems so cruel a fashion
at times. This is also why she teases Dimmesdale, for in him she notes a
bashfulness very much like the shame-encouraged reticence in her
mother. She acts haughtily to Dimmesdale when he acts as a religious
leader of the community which never ceased reminding Hester of her sin,
but she acts in tenderness to the same man when he resembles the guilt
shown by Hester.

If shame brings out the good and bad in the life-loving daughter of
Hester, it only brings out the bad in Hester's secret husband, Chillingworth. Like the community at large, the doctor uses guilt-feelings to further the torments of the supposedly guilty. As Dimmesdale sinks unto
deeper remorse, the doctor's only reaction is to heap more coals upon his
head, and the physician not only succeeds in the death of Dimmesdale
through shame, he also succeeds in killing himself in the process. Once
Dimmesdale is vanquished, there is nothing else for the doctor to live
for. He could not, even if he wished, touch Hester because she has managed to convert and strenghten her personality through this horrible
guilt, and he could not hurt Pearl, because by nature and upbringing
she has come to repel any feeling of this overwhelming shame in her interior life.

As has been mentioned, Dimmesdale and Chillingworth express very
similar philosophies of life, and it is obvious in their actions that both
men relish guilt to abnormal degrees. The doctor pursues guilt in the
hidden lover because he wishes revenge. However it is likely he pursues
it because he also senses that he has been an inadequate husband both
sexually and emotionally. Dimmesdale also hungers for occasion to intensify his guilt. He does not have the courage to speak out, even at his
death, and so he seeks those things, fasting, self-scourging, pseudo-con-
fessional sermons, which will remind him further of his sinfulness.

If shame ruins the men, it does not do so to the two women (if we may
call Pearl that for the moment). As mentioned Pearl lives outside the
limits of shame. She grows up to spite it. Hester grows also. She becomes
the tragic heroine largely because she allows shame to work in her, to
change her, but not to pervert her. Hawthorne is being quite consistent

when he favors this fortitude in the females of *The Scarlet Letter*. If you remember, it was the women at the prison door at the story's start who seemed to be stronger and more self-willed than the men. Those beefy women, sturdy as the good queen Bess of a generation before, wanted the rigorous punishment and shouted the loudest when Hester got off so lightly. Hester is lovely and elegant, especially in comparison to these women folk, but she is as tough as they are. She too is a daughter of the good queen, and that is why there is something left when shame runs its course.

What the sense of sin and shame does to the community at large is even more terrifying than what it does to the men. We do not see the Salem mind at work very often in very specific acts. This is not a novel primarily dealing with New England mores and morality. However what we do see of shame at work in the community at large is not very attractive. Youngsters seem to be as tainted with the spirit of revenge as Chillingworth. The adults seem always to be standing in front of that scaffold, huddled in dark, murmuring groups and staring at some sinner. Their life as a community seems to be lived apart from joy in a prison of speculation on evil and its consequences. Someone is always sinning or about to sin, and evil is everywhere. It is as physically present as the church, the prison, the graveyard; indeed each one of these places seems to be a symbol for the others. Sin and shame are preached in church, are punished in the prison and on the scaffold; and the graveyard harbors the temporally punished victims of this mass conscience when life is ended.

It is important to notice that the community is first and forever identified with these places, not with the chat by the fireside or with walks in the forest or on the common lawn. The community ill-uses Hester in her shame because they live in shame, in a common sense of spiritual misgivings about themselves and the world at large. Historically, Salemites believed in witches and witches' sabbaths because an extreme form of guilt had tainted the common conscience and imagination, and the same is true for the Salem of our novel. Mistress Hibbins is a witch or near witch because sin, or rather a sense of sin, overpowered an already weakened mind and soul—and the same is true for Dimmesdale and Chillingworth. However the sensibility was not completely self-created. Pearl is ample testimony that we arrive emotionally whole. Mistress Hibbins and the others have been infected with the community's sense of inadequacy. She and the major male characters collapse because of it; Hester dies and is born again.

As the novel nears its dramatic ending, the private sinners and the shame-loving community come together for a final testimony for the sense of shame that runs through every conscience and touches on every conversation. What the Salemites are seeing are three adults ruined by shame in one way or another and a child who has been made an outcast as a consequence of it. These very distinctive people stand before all now as an embodiment of the Salem mind in its own shame. The great tragedy is that the community cannot see the import of it all. They cannot see that this is truly their family, their general offspring. Hawthorne in writing the last scaffold scene takes us up to the platform and lets us hear the voice of the four people there. In this climax we must remember it takes place in public before the entire community. The puzzlement and the general uproar is going on as the four stand on the platform, and the confusion of voices we hear at Dimmesdale's death is a result of the general spiritual pessimism that has kept the Salemites from looking lovingly and honestly at life since the founding of the community. The community as a body cannot accept the responsibility of the four standing above them, because shame has kept it from acting clearly and objectively about anything.

CHARACTER ANALYSIS

The Community

Through one interpretation or another, it is always possible to arrive at some understanding and, at times, sympathy for the major characters in the work. Hester, Chillingworth, Dimmesdale, and Pearl are given to us with a great deal of description and motivation, and for those reasons we feel they have, at their various times, varying degrees of reasonable action; and they, insofar as they are made real, are able to be appreciated. Not so for the mass of people in the background. At the opening of the story, they wait in almost malicious glee for the punished Hester. When they discover the light sentence they are dissatisfied. The women especially seem vengeful and brutelike. As the story progresses, there is little progress in their sympathy for Hester; indeed they have none. They are willing to have her daughter taken from her, and their children, aping this antagonism, are all to willing to muddy Hester and Pearl.

As Hester grows to the new womanhood she so hurtfully earned, the community does not forgive, it forgets. Hester earns a new reputation, but the sense of sin held by these folk takes, it seems, forever to die. At the last scaffold scene where Dimmesdale confesses his guilt, what we now see is not the vengeful crowd, but the confused mob. Hawthorne here has no need to exemplify a trait of perverseness seen earlier, but what he does show is equally distasteful as far as the community is concerned; they seem, as a group, to be as confused over Dimmesdale's purpose and Chillingworth's leering as they once were certain of Hester's guilt. Pearl has to leave Salem because she is not of their kind, which is to say that the community is as repugnant to her nature as it was deadly to Hester and the two men in her life. Because of the general malignancy the crowd either sponsored or cultivated, the two men were helped to their rather grotesque ends, and Hester died twice: once to the new and subdued woman we see in the story and finally in physical passing; she was happy for her daughter's new position, but could never forget an earlier time. Surely, Hester's continuing to wear the "A" on her dress is indication that the taint of sin and guilt was still in the community.

The sense of sin carried by the principal characters certainly does make the tale of the letter a dark one. However, if you consider the crowd in all of its actions, you will see that it is the people as a whole which make the tale such a sorrowful and diabolical one. They truly create the atmosphere of purposeful futility which opens and closes the book. Even the oldsters in the Custom House chapter contribute to this general sickness. They are not dangerous as the earlier Salemites are, but they are useless and cliquish, and almost unreal. It would seem that our story teller had to escape from them in order to create. And it is true that he is inspired by an individual ghost from the past, and by this collection of near-ghosts of the present.

Hawthorne, in this story and in most of his other works, has been found to be an extremely pessimistic depictor of the human condition; and if we consider, as we have here been doing, how he looks at people in mass, we can see some justification for this view. Individuals seem to overcome by dint of some great courage, as in the case of Hester, but the crowd never does. It seems to harbor an infectious guilt. It is the crowd which is the vengeful god. In *The Scarlet Letter,* Dimmesdale and Chillingworth are the living manifestations of the community's own perverse nature. Dimmesdale is adored and respected by them because he suffers and speaks penance. True, they do not know the final import of his various sermons, but they relish his discomfort nonetheless because this is their norm of spirituality: something weak, pale, and suffering. They try his supposed goodness by yoking him with a devil; many in the community feel that Chillingworth's purpose is to further purify the already long-suffering character of the minister by more torment. Although some in the community suspect Chillingworth's nature, they still accept him as their physician. And the thwarted doctor is enough a part of the community to whisper advice in the governor's ear when that man is considering whether Hester should keep Pearl.

After weighing the general character of the community, one can ask again what is the purpose of all of Hester's suffering? Hawthorne cannot offer any final answer. Our only solace, amidst the general depravity of the people at large and their children is to notice that Pearl is a happy result of the communal despair. Hester proves that one can survive under conditions of common perversity, and Pearl proves that some singular good exists.

The Presence of Chillingworth

The reader learns in the opening chapters that Hester's husband, a man much older than she, had left her years before. He had been held captive by the Indians but has also fed "the hungry dreams of knowledge" in study of alchemy; the "devourer of great libraries" had had no time for a young, vibrant wife. The man suddenly reappears, a stranger in the crowd as Hester emerges from the prison. When he sees the girl with the child that is not his own, "a writhing horror" twists across his face. After he has taken the name Chillingworth, become Salem's physician and

Dimmesdale's "medical advisor," torturing and probing the minister's soul, the vengeant husband's appearance grows more and more horrible. "The former aspect of an intellectual and studious man, calm and quiet, ... had altogether vanished, and been succeeded by an eager, searching, almost fierce, yet carefully guarded look"; "there came a glare of red light out of his eyes, as if the old man's soul were on fire. . . ." Roger Chillingworth is developed from an idea which appears in Hawthorne's notebooks in 1847: "a study of the effects of revenge, in diabolizing him who indulges in it."

Hawthorne was deeply concerned with the paradox of Puritanism: social *morality* is demanded of members of the religious community while the religion itself assumes as dogma the essentially *sinful* nature of all men. "In Adam's fall we sinned all," repeats the schoolboy's primer, and yet there seems no one in the community in the first chapter reluctant not to "cast the first stone." The paradox is manifest in Hester openly wearing her shame upon her breast, and Dimmesdale concealing his own guilt. Such hypocritical condemnation of evil as the community's (and Dimmesdale's, *qua* minister) serves only to deepen the fault, to intensify the evil itself. Chillingworth may be seen as representative of this corrupting influence.

The thwarted doctor's satanic personality pervades the novel as the satanism he comes to stand for pervades Salem. His power affects the interrelationships of all the major characters and it is thus in examination of these that his literary function is to be clarified.

Hester's Sin

Paradoxically, Hawthorne's work is one of the most asexual books to have ever treated or worked with what was originally a sexual action. Hester's spiritual offense as far as the community is concerned is adultery, but strangely enough we do not think of any one specific offense once we are a few chapters into *The Scarlet Letter*. Somehow, even before Hawthorne begins overlaying her action with all sorts of allegorical meanings, the reader merely thinks of Hester as one who has sinned, not as one who sinned with a man.

A similar transformation happens in our regard for the folk of Salem and the locale of all this action. Why is it that a novel with specific historical references to real people (e.g., the governors) and real places refuses to be left as a plain history? Why is it that the Puritans as a specific Christian sect become non-denominational the more we read and reread the work? The answer must be that Hawthorne's theme is so immediately universal that it shrugs off any permanent suggestion of one time and place. Hester's spiritual crime then is really Eve's sin, and Salem is another Eden, the Eden after the fall. Consider then some of the minor suggestions in the story which bolster an interpretation of *The Scarlet Letter* in this light.

Chillingworth lurks everywhere ready to tempt his already fallen victim with more error. Young Pearl, until the final scaffold scene, is often likened to an angel containing and carrying the truth about hypocrisies and satanic purposes; in the beginning of the story the narrator says that she enacts a guilelessness devoid of any sin or conventional morality: she is unfallen and only serves to show how fallen are the others. In the Genesis story Adam and Eve trade innocence for a knowledge of good and evil; in *The Scarlet Letter* Hester's love affair with Dimmesdale precipitates a new sense of guilt and shame for all as well as a new sense of love. Hester knows intuitively the evil around her, and Dimmesdale knows more than he can bear of the interior evil of his hypocrisy.

One of the paradoxes of the Genesis tale is that while man lost one of his virtues, he also enlarged his knowledge and so gained attributes. Hester's passionate regard for life and her vitality is lost through her adultery, but she becomes a ministering angel as a consequence; despite all the machinations of Salem's satan, some good has come from the evil. To begin to see how much the fall of Hester resembles the fall of man in Biblical literature is to see how Hawthorne is not so much concerned with seventeenth-century Salem as he is with the general notion of guilt and sin as it happens to be demonstrated in a specific action.

Dimmesdale's Conscience

The commentaries here have been very critical of Dimmesdale's spiritual and psychological nature. But it would be folly to think that this writer's opinion is the last word in this matter. Hawthorne's work is both wide and deep, and the huge and ever-growing bibliography on this novel is testimony enough that there are other interpretations. Several facts can lend themselves to a more sympathetic attitude towards the man. In a few places the narrator mentions that the younger women of the community had both a spiritual and romantic affection for Dimmesdale; what they believed to be a respect for Dimmesdale's venerable reputation was in part a physical and emotional attachment to a young ascetic. Although it is never stated explicitly in the work, Hester's initial response to Dimmesdale could have been of the same kind. So, there was some suggestion of passion and masculinity in the earlier Dimmesdale, and the narrator says as much in his first description of the man's features.

Hester notes in the forest meeting that Pearl is his child as well as hers and that the girl's character demonstrates this. Realizing now Pearl's own unconventional vivacity and her lovely features, one can say that Dimmesdale was earlier something more than a trembling hypocrite. Again the more we value Hester, first in her former audacious self and later in the new wisdom she acquires, remembering her constant (but fluctuating) regard for Dimmesdale, the more we might say that there was a more lively and honest part to Dimmesdale. Chillingworth at the meeting in the Governor's house notices the attractive nature of Pearl and claims that some of this must have come from her unknown father. These are a few of the more obvious reasons for some critics claiming a one-time stronger and more manly nature in Dimmesdale.

There is then at least one alternative if we wish to have a less skeptical regard for the minister. One can claim that Dimmesdale's initial disintegration and reversal of character takes place before the novel proper begins, or during Hester's trial, and that Hawthorne, preferring to concentrate on Hester's predicament in the early part, merely gives us the clues about Dimmesdale as are mentioned above. The difficulty that this reader sees, however, is that the change in Dimmesdale's alleged earlier nature, even before he meets his deadly physician, is so fantastic that there must have been very little character to counter this guilt to start with. However, there is one other retort to even this last conclusion: the sense of guilt that pervades the community is so formidable that, if it can conquer Hester and make another woman of her, it could do the same to Dimmesdale, who could have been equally strong in character at one time.

There is one short story written several years before *The Scarlet Letter* which provides a touchstone to understanding Dimmesdale in a more favorable light. "Young Goodman Brown" (1835) is about a young and trusting man who loses his faith in himself and all about him after a meeting (real or imagined) with an evil spirit and this being's alleged converts. Several of his converts are venerated members of the community; one taught Brown his religion lessons, others were ministers; and finally Brown imagines he sees his wife Faith present at the satanic initiation ceremony. This convinces him that evil is the only potent force in life. When he returns to his community, he is a completely disillusioned and cynical man, and he eventually dies a shrivelled old man with no true companion but his gloom. Before this fateful journey, Brown had been asked by his young and pretty wife Faith not to go out alone on that dreary night lest something happen to him. He persists and has his terrible conversion. The point should be clear: once a man separates himself even briefly from faith touched with an optimistic and lively regard for all things, he is lost. Dimmesdale could have easily had such a positive approach to life at one time, even had it been quietly and bookishly expressed, only to be separated from it in the freely-willed adultery with Hester. Once he chooses to leave her and go his own hidden way, a gloom similar to Brown's is all that can follow.

Young Goodman Brown and his simplistic faith cannot be left bathed in the light of this interpretation, for there are many things in the short story which lead one to devalue the man as much as has been done in the chapter commentaries on Dimmesdale. The man that Brown meets seems very much like him, and so there is good indication that the tempter is a weakness latent in Brown. Once Brown travels in the company of the man, he seems all too willing to believe the worst of people he has loved and respected. If he honestly realized that evil is deceptive and cunning in its nature, as he claims, there should be every reason to doubt the accuracy of his visions. On setting out, Brown speaks of his wife in endearing terms, but his manner of expression is touched with a certain manly arrogance; in short even in his respect for a loved one there is the suggestion of a flaw. Even if Brown's character may be morally inclined, it is still weakened by a self-willed over-confidence and a deliberate pessimism, and who is to say he had very far to fall, the supposed cunning of the tempter notwithstanding. A similar question may be asked of Dimmesdale. How much temptation did his already debased character need to bring it to its final destination?

Hawthorne is a master writer because he can encourage one reaction which works against another. What these contrary interpretations demonstrate is the paradox of evil, real or imagined, and guilt concerning evil actions. To Hawthorne, evil and a sense of it existed. Perhaps one was the same as the other; he leaves that for us, in our own natures, to decide. But even if he cannot claim to finally know the origins and causes of evil and guilt, he certainly does a marvelous job of showing man undergoing and perhaps causing the torments of this mystery. Evil in Dimmesdale is as much of a mystery as Hester's love for this man is. One principle seems certain, no matter what regard one finally has for Dimmesdale, evil and a destroying pessimism for Hawthorne's creatures functions unhampered where there is no love. Hester's does not make her a joyous woman, but she survives. The Prioress in *The Canterbury Tales* wore a golden brooch on her habit; its figure "A" stood for the motto *Amor vincit omnia*, "Love overcomes all things." Hester's "A" signifies nearly as much.

Pearl and Her Role

The synopsis and commentary in the preceding sections should give a very clear idea of who Pearl is. In spirit she is her mother's child, not

Dimmesdale's; however her traits come from the Hester before the trial, the passionate and life-giving woman who is sacrificed at the altar of a community's wrath. By associating Pearl with Biblical and profane personages, Hawthorne not only shows a very complex young girl reacting within this tense and forbidding environment, he also shows the forces of life and death, joy in life and sorrow under a Puritan god, as well as the angelic and satanic elements which go to make up the characters of Hester and Chillingworth respectively. This suggestion of forces from one character is an admirable artistic feat, and Hawthorne carries it off masterfully. Pearl is called a "demon offspring," a prankish assistant to the master of revels, and an "elfin creature" among other profane references. These show us the unconventional and rebellious creature who can tease the cowardly Dimmesdale, scatter in furious screaming the Puritan children, and act saucily to the greybeards who wish to remove her from her mother's care. In these situations, Pearl is a healthy contrast to the pessimism in the community, and her personality touches a sad story with hope: not everyone will succumb to a fatal sense of inferiority; fortunately there are some who believe they are created in God's image and not in Satan's. Paradoxically, the profane associations with Pearl show us the optimistic side to Christian belief in man under God.

Pearl is also likened to the precious jewel mentioned in the gospel of Matthew (xiii. 45-46). Precious, she *has* been purchased at great price —great sacrifice would be more accurate. This Pearl of Matthew is the angelic creature who has been isolated by a wrathful community; this is the Pearl who loves, and does not tease, her mother, and sobs on the bosom of her dying father. Strangely enough, this aspect of Pearl, though touched with Christian associations, emphasizes as much sorrow and vice as the profane associations stress the good. Pearl as Matthew's jewel makes us think of sacrifice first, not joy. Hawthorne in his references has made them crisscross, each suggesting its apparent opposite. The profane becomes honest joy under God and the Biblical becomes sorrow, pessimism, and the general wrathful character sponsored by Chillingworth and Dimmesdale.

Because Pearl is tossed between the polarities of life and death, joy and sorrow, she can act extremely, or seem to act so in any event. The tensions around her are so powerful as to encourage powerful reply. Hawthorne says in so many words that there are many Pearls and that she can slip from one to the other as quickly as sun and clouds cause light or shadows on a windy summer day. Even when Pearl may be acting quite normally, she may seem to act abnormally because of the point of view of the onlookers. Hester sees much of her previous nature in Pearl, and she sees the child as a constant reminder of her (Hester's) fall from grace. Under these circumstances, it is no wonder that every action of Pearl, no matter what its intention or real nature, is seen and interpreted with magnification. The same is true of Dimmesdale's reaction to the girl; he sees the past before him, and it is not surprising that Pearl can make him speechless and frightened in more than his usual shyness whenever she moves a finger.

Chillingworth's reaction to Pearl is the most amazing of all. He seems to harbor no intense ill-feeling toward the girl, yet Pearl is the embodiment of a passion and fecundity the lame doctor could not himself muster. It is indeed strange that this love-child is not distasteful to the man who seems to hate so easily. Admittedly, if he did actively hate Pearl, Chillingworth would be so despicable as to be unreal. But why not disdain, and why does he leave his estate to her? The answer must be love —love for Hester or for Pearl, or for both of them. And if this is the case, then Chillingworth, though satanic in his other accomplishments, is still in some small and flickering way human and humane. In leaving his estate to Pearl, he must be saying he still holds affection for Hester or that he sees goodness in this unconventional love-child, and he wishes to protect it and her from the pessimism which has ruled and ruined his own life.

By now it should be clear that not only is Pearl a complicated being who functions well in the story, but that she also serves as a touchstone for evaluating in another way the characters of the people with which she comes in contact. To examine Hester's attitude toward Pearl is to know Hester better, and the same is true for Dimmesdale. Moreover, to consider as we have been doing, the response of Chillingworth to Pearl is to again note what was mentioned earlier about that man: he is entirely human and he does preserve some chance for goodness never fully realized. He shows as much by providing for Pearl. In so doing he condemns himself and the community which allowed him to operate so easily. In spite of his weakened introspective attitudes towards life, he is praising vivacity.

Although the idea may seem unusual, there is now valid reason for implying that *The Scarlet Letter* is as much about Pearl as anyone. Of all the characters in the story she is the most complicated, and considering her years with her experience, it is easy to see that she has greater force of character than any other single person. If you recall the places where she is mentioned, you will realize how impressive is her role. Not only does she help us evaluate those considering her, she also projects a powerful personality in her own right. Indeed, it is just as easy to say that the others exist to show through their reaction how and what Pearl is. Because she is a child in all of the narration up to the concluding chapter, one tends to assign her a minor role in this adult tragedy. That is conventional and illogical. We meet her as soon as we do Hester, and she occupies as much narrative attention as Hester. Viewed so, *The Scarlet Letter,* is much more than a story of a woman who survives, it is a joyous shout for the unconventional and spontaneous reaction and for honesty. The adults in *The Scarlet Letter* all die. Pearl lives in new estate in England at the start of a great age of scientific and philosophical discovery. She is the child of a *new* testament, still Christian, but now confident.

QUESTIONS AND ANSWERS

1. **Analyze the differences between the 'old' and 'new' Hester.**

   Your answer should not only be concerned with actions of the heroine, such as a previous impetuousity shown in her love affair and
   her later submissiveness in the face of the community's scorn, but
   also you should show how natural objects and events associated with
   her person by the narrator (the wild rose at the prison door) become
   displaced by such natural phenomena as clouds and shadows. In
   short, Hester's interior change is demonstrated not only by her appearance and her new sympathies, but by her connection with the
   physical world in nature.

2. **Describe the narrator's regard for public opinion and the fickleness
   of conventional morality.**

   There are many places in the work where the storyteller shows the
   variety of public opinion. The last chapter is one of the most ironically presented examples of the unreasonable personality of a mob.
   It is one of the few places where the narrator becomes quite bitter
   in his description. However, the same is true in earlier places, such
   as the scene outside the prison (Chapters II and III) where the group
   is presented in an unfavorable, or at least unattractive light, or the
   description of and reaction to the meteor which appears on the night
   of the second scaffold scene (Chapter XII).

3. **Discuss the variety of ways in which young Pearl's fortunes change.**

   Even the innocent undergo important transformations in the heat of
   the guilt and sorrows of others. Pearl becomes a full human being
   in giving her love to the dying Dimmesdale (Chapter XXIII), and
   she, through her mother's freedom, can travel abroad and begin a
   life of her own. However, she does lose something. She can never
   hope to have the companionship of her loving and heroic mother.
   In her isolated childhood she has an individuality and vitality which
   enables her to dance on the graves of the Puritan dead and throw
   mud at the Governor. In leaving her environment, these attributes
   are no longer needed, at least in that degree. Does she risk becoming
   conventional? Naturally no one would wish Pearl to stay to inherit
   the sorrow of her mother, but you will have to realize that Pearl's
   individuality is in some way diminished. What then does she inherit from Chillingworth and Dimmesdale besides money and the
   chance at a normal life?

4. Show how isolation, both physical and psychological, affects the major characters in *The Scarlet Letter*.

Newton Arvin in *Hawthorne* (1929) suggests a key to Hawthorne's attitude towards the solitary: "Mark the form that guiltiness habitually takes in his (Hawthorne's) representation of it, and you will be in no doubt of its origin. The essential sin, he would seem to say, lies in whatever shuts up the spirit in a dungeon where it is alone, beyond the reach of common sympathies and the general sunlight. All that isolates, damns; all that associates, saves." What does Hester's stay in the prison do to her? Dimmesdale locks himself within his guilt and refuses himself any honest communication with the congregation. Chillingworth also operates in the dark and in secret. And Pearl, though sharing some association with her mother, lives outside the world. The effect of these various seclusions creates various difficulties for the major characters, and your analysis should distinguish them.

5. At least one critic has noted that Hawthorne, being both the product of a Puritan heritage and a free-thinking man, was forced to choose between the ideal of personal freedom and personal communion with God (the optimistic side of Puritan doctrine) and the overwhelming sense of a corruptable and sinful human being (the pessimistic aspect of Puritan belief). Is such a choice made in *The Scarlet Letter?*

One must weigh the full and final effect of Hester's initial residence in Salem and her final return. Has she succeeded in maintaining herself once her sin is discovered or re-creating her individuality once Dimmesdale dies? Also one must choose some set attitude towards Dimmesdale's motives in his confession. Is his action freely willed, and, if it is, does this act of personal freedom enable him to escape guilt or merely the torments of Chillingworth? Pearl has escaped the Salem community and lives a new life which we can assume is free from the oppressive guilt which hurt her mother. However, is Pearl's new life a victory over the religious sense of sin in one community or merely a removal from it? How pertinent is *The Scarlet Letter* to our own everyday lives?

6. Vernon Parrington in his chapter on Hawthorne in *Main Currents in American Thought* (1927) did not feel that Hawthorne had any hold on the real world and its problems: "He was the extreme and finest expression of the refined alienation from reality that in the end palsied the creative mind of New England." Hawthorne's work is an allegorical romance and by definition is working through an

illusory and unworldly atmosphere. However, does Hawthorne's concentration on the interior problems of the characters, his use of unusual occurrences such as meteors and vanishing sunlight, and the presence of people like Mistress Hibbins and Pearl and Chillingworth, who seem to possess unusual intuitions, make his story so unreal that it cannot be related to the joys and pleasures of our own world?

The answer to Parrington's objection involves an important belief in how far an author can use the unreal and improbable to create a dramatic and pertinent literary situation. Does the narrator in *The Scarlet Letter* ever state explicitly that the strange occurrences really happened? How much of the very specific details in Hester's story does the narrator hold to?

RESEARCH AREAS

Freudian Analysis   All of the major characters can be discussed in psychoanalytic terms. Using the guidelines established by Simon O. Lesser in his *Fiction and the Unconscious* (1957), consider how Hester manifests her repressed desire for her former life in the way she dresses young Pearl. Decide if Dimmesdale and Chillingworth go to the religious and rationalistic lengths they do manage to achieve because libidinous energy ordinarily associated with sexual ends has been diverted through the pressures of society or some physical defect. Does Dimmesdale show any of the characteristics of the Oedipus complex in the way he reacts generally to women and specifically with Pearl and Hester?

Social Analysis   Although the novel was written over a hundred years ago about a community in seventeenth-century America, can the same or similar social and moral taboos be still observed in the towns and cities of America? Using your personal experiences or sociological studies you can decide if the contemporary place in question is still sensitive to the forces at play at the time of Hester. Are illegitimate children still seen in this same light? Do children from broken or estranged families grow up abnormally? Do people of religious congregations still build extraordinary myths about their religious representatives? Are there still super-rationalistic creatures, would-be scientists like Chillingworth who delight in undermining what may be the honest faith of a community? There is no general answer possible to this sort of examination; one must be very specific and refer to very detailed social situations.

Religious Analysis   It is possible to decide from the novel how much or how little the narrator held to a religious view of the world? Are his supernatural events within the realm of possibility in the context of the tale? Dimmesdale may have many flaws, but does the way in which his character is dilineated in any way suggest that religion is a worthless activity? Again, your answer must be balanced and exact. Hester is not an active member of the congregation, but she exhibits great charity, and the narrator does compare her with a great religious leader. Moreover Pearl is likened to the Biblical pearl of Matthew (see glossary). In spite of his apparent cynicism, may the narrator be an extremely religious man?

BIBLIOGRAPHY

What follows here is a starter list for anyone unfamiliar with Hawthorne's life and major works. *Eight American Authors: A Review of Research and Criticism,* edited by Floyd Stovall, 1962, (a Norton paperback) contains a descriptive bibliography of Hawthorne scholarship to that time and this may be supplemented by the annual bibliography of the Modern Language Association.

Editions

The Complete Works, 12 vols., edited by G. P. Lathrop, 1883, has been the standard edition, but there are superior editions of separate and selected works.

The Scarlet Letter and Other Tales of the Puritans, edited by Harry Levin (Riverside Editions: 1961), has sufficient footnotes and a good introduction.

The Scarlet Letter, edited by Sculley Bradley (A Norton Critical Edition: 1962), contains the novel and several interesting essays on Hawthorne and this work. This text and the one previous are the best student editions available.

The Portable Hawthorne, edited by Malcolm Cawley (Viking Press: 1948), has well-chosen stories and a worthwhile introduction.

The American Notebooks of Nathanial Hawthorne, edited by Randall Stewart (1932), is invaluable for seeing how Hawthorne transformed fact and antiquarian lore into literature.

Biography

Hawthorne, by George E. Woodbury (1902), is the most factual life studies to date.

Hawthorne, by Newton Arvin (1929), is a psychologically oriented biography concerned with Hawthorne's extreme preoccupation with guilt and the dangers of excessive introspection.

Nathanial Hawthorne: A Bibliography, by Randall Stewart (1948), is a short but important study which has led to the modern reevaluation of the man and his work.

Essays on *The Scarlet Letter* and Related Ideas

"Pearl and the Puritan Heritage," C. E. Eisinger (*College English:* 1951).

"Hawthorne's Psychology of the Head and Heart," D. A. Ringe (*Publications of the Modern Language Association:* 1950).

"Hawthorne's Hester and Feminism," N. F. Doubleday (*PMLA:* 1939).

"Hawthorne and Romantic Love and the Status of Women," Morton Cronin (*PMLA:* 1954).

"Hawthorne and Puritan Punishments," G. H. Orians (*CE:* 1952).

American Renaissance, F. O. Matthiessen (1941). Contains invaluable commentary on *The Scarlet Letter.*

"Form and Content in *The Scarlet Letter,*" J. C. Gerber (*New England Quarterly,* 1944).

"*The Scarlet Letter* and Its Modern Critics," C. C. Walcutt (*Nineteenth-Century Fiction:* 1953).

"Hawthorne's Dimmesdale: Fugitive from Wrath," Darrel Abel (*NCF:* 1956)

"Motivation in *The Scarlet Letter,*" E. C. Sampson (*American Literature:* 1957).

GLOSSARY

Persons, Places, and Events

The elder Adams is John Adams (1735—1826), second President of the United States; his son, John Quincy Adams, was the sixth President.

Amos Bronson Alcott (1799—1888), father of the novelist Louisa May Alcott, was a transcendental philosopher and educational reformer.

Assabeth is a river near Concord, Massachusetts.

Francis Bacon (1561—1626), for a while Lord Chancellor of England, was the practical creator of the inductive method and the father of the modern scientific attitude. His two best known and most influential works are *The Advancement of Learning* (1605) and the *Novum Organum* (1620). Aside from an astonishing career as a philosophical writer, Bacon was also adviser to James I and a master of the intrigues of court. Late in his career, he was fined and briefly imprisoned for taking bribes and using his position wrongly; he died as a result of a cold caught while making experiments to see the effect of refrigeration on meat.

Richard Bellingham (1592—1672), an English-born lawyer, came to Boston in 1634. He was three times governor of the colony.

Reverend Mr. Blackstone, as Hawthorne notes, was supposedly the first white settler in the area around Boston. The legends about him suggest he disliked the Puritans and rode off to live with the Indians when the Puritan settlers arrived. The fact that he rides a bull connotes that his own free and virile attitude towards life is a healthy contrast to the staid Salemites.

The Black Man is Satan or his representative. Pearl calls both Chillingworth and Dimmesdale such in the story, and Mistress Hibbins is said to have "signed his book" or made a pact with him for her soul in exchange for certain magical powers. In the story, after we first see him in the cell with Hester, Chillingworth is made to seem very much this demonic figure so popular in medieval and Puritan folklore. The Black Man is often associated with the "witches' sabbath," a demonic religious service where a congregation of witches and others devoted to Satan gather to worship.

The Horn Book was a sheet of parchment with the alphabet, table of numbers, and the like on it, mounted on a small board with a handle and covered with a layer of transparent horn.

Boreas is the god of the north wind; he is traditionally depicted as being of a blustery and aggressive nature.

Simon Bradstreet (1603—1697), was an early governor in New England.

Brook Farm was the title given the communal, agrarian project near Boston begun by the Transcendentalists in the 1840's.

Robert Burns (1759-1796), the famous Scottish poet, received a royal appointment as district collector of taxes in 1789.

Cain was the first murderer (Genesis iv, 1-16); his forehead was branded by God so that the world, knowing he was a killer, would not kill him in turn.

Geoffrey Chaucer (1340—1400), the author of *The Canterbury Tales,* had been a customs official among his many other royal appointments.

Change is the familiar name of the Boston Merchant's Exchange.

William Ellery Channing was a friend of Ralph Waldo Emerson and a Transcendentalist.

Chippewa and *Fort Erie* are decisive battles which General Miller, "the brave soldier" of "The Custom House" fought in during the War of 1812.

Chronicles of England, or Holinshed's *Chronicles of England, Scotland and Ireland* (1577) was a well-known Elizabethan history of those countries, their customs and heroes. Shakespeare, among other writers, took characters and incidents from its pages as material for his plays.

Edward Coke (1552—1634), famous jurist and member of Parliament, did much to protect and strengthen the national liberties against the attempts of the Crown and Church to abridge them. He was a political enemy of Francis Bacon and did much to bring the man to justice for his illegal practices. His classic *Reports* and *Institutes* are important legal commentaries on the rights of tenure, criminal law, statutes, and the jurisdictions of various courts of law.

Daniel, the prophet, read the fatal handwriting seen on a wall during the arrogant King Belshazzar's feast: "Thou art weighed in the balance and found wanting" (Daniel v). Chillingworth is asked by a member of the community gathered before the scaffold to guess as to the parentage of Pearl. He does spend the rest of his unnatural life trying to "read" her origins and punish her father once he sees what he imagines to be an "A" on the breast of Dimmesdale. Chillingworth is very much like an unholy prophet of doom in the story, and this allusion to Daniel establishes this part of his role.

David and *Bathsheba* and *Nathan the Prophet* are principals in the famous love story of David. He sent Uriah, Bathsheba's husband, to a fatal war engagement so that he could have the woman for himself. Nathan told David that he was despised in God's eyes and that his first son would die for that adulterous murder. See II Samuel xi and xii.

Demon offspring. In medieval folklore and the lore held by the Puritans, it was believed that diabolic spirits begot lawless and wild offspring upon unsuspecting women. Pearl is likened to one of these children by many people in the story, and many times Pearl encourages this belief to separate herself from the Salem community and its rigorous morality.

King Derby or *Elias Hasket Derby* (1739–1799) outfitted and armed his own ships for the colonial side during the Revolution.

Sir Kenelm Digby (1603–1665), privateer and favorite of Charles I and II, discovered that oxygen was necessary to sustain plant life. He was one of the first members of the Royal Society and a friend of Descartes as well as a writer of bombast.

Dig gold in California, in "The Custom House" section, is a reference to the California gold rush in 1849.

Dragon's teeth were cast on the ground by the mythical Cadmus, and they took root and grew to become armed men. They fought until only five were left, and these helped the Phoenician prince to build the city of Thebes.

Thomas Dudley (1576–1653) was an early governor in New England.

The earliest immigrant of my name is a reference to William Hathorne who came to Massachusetts in 1630. Nathaniel, the author, added the 'w' to the family name. Magistrate John Hathorne, son of the first American Hathorne, was a judge in the witchcraft trials held in Salem in 1692.

John Elliot (1604-1690), the "Indian Apostle," was a graduate of Jesus College, Cambridge; in 1631 he left England and within a few years had begun to preach to Indians at Nonatum in their dialect; soon afterwards he established "praying towns" or communities for his Indian converts, and by 1674 there were nearly 4,000 of these Christianized Indians. Aside from various translations of religious works to Indian dialects, Elliot helped prepare *The Bay Psalm Book*, the first book printed in New England.

Elixir of Life is a supposedly magical substance that can convert worthless metals to gold and cure any and all sicknesses.

Man-like Elizabeth is, of course, the vigorous and outspoken Elizabeth I (1558—1603) who reigned during one of the greatest periods in English history. The "virgin queen" was no maiden meek and mild and so seems, in part, a fitting national ancestress for the hardy women folk waiting for Hester to quit the prison. Elizabeth had a great intelligence and amazing political talent, but these qualities are not part of the association made by Hawthorne with the Puritan females.

John Endicott (1588—1665) was governor of the Massachusetts Colony.

Enoch, the eldest son of Cain and father of Methuselah, was raised to Heaven without dying; he "walked with God; and he was not, for God took him," Genesis v, 24.

John Finch (1584—1660), *Baron Finch,* was a famous English jurist.

Five-fingers is the common starfish.

Doctor Forman. See Sir Thomas Overbury.

Simon Forrester (1776—1854) was considered to be one of the wealthiest men in the Salem area.

Gobelin looms are those of the family of dyers and weavers that began a famous tapestry factory on the outskirts of Paris about the middle of the 15th century.

Old Bill Gray (1750—1825) had been lieutenant governor of Massachusetts.

Henbane. See nightshade.

George Stillam Hill(i)ard 1808—1879 was a wealthy Bostonian, prominent in literary circles and a friend and adviser to Hawthorne.

Horse-shoe is the horseshoe crab.

Mrs. Anne Hutchinson (1590—1643), the famed colonial evangelist was born in Lincolnshire, England. When she was in her early twenties she married and several years later emigrated with her husband to Boston. She felt that the colonial clergy were far more concerned with promulgating laws and procedures regulating conduct than they were with the interior life of their flocks and the personal character of the individual soul. She believed that one is redeemed by the quality of one's soul in faith and the spirit of the gospel message and not by the proscriptions of clergy, and she began preaching as much. She was tried for sedition and heresy and banished. After a few years in Rhode Island in a democratic settlement started with lands acquired from the Narragansett Indians, she moved to New York State. In less than a year, she, now a widow, and all of her family, but one son, were murdered by local Indians.

Hawthorne associated Hester with Anne Hutchinson in at least two places in the novel, and rather than simply fortify and complement the heroic stature of our heroine, the conjunction seems to illustrate what great sacrifices Hester makes and what terrific changes take place in Hester as a result of these sacrifices. Anne was a fiery religious enthusiast, Hester is anything but that after her sentence. Hester's example is created in silence and sadness, not so with Anne. Both women have great strength of character, but realizing how different are their strengths and their characters is to see how painful Hester's lot in life is and what great vivacity has been suppressed in her life after the trial.

Irving's Headless Horseman is an allusion to Washington Irving's "The Legend of Sleepy Hollow." In the story, Ichabod Crane, a frail, timid, but all the same pompous school teacher, is frightened out of town by Brom Bones masquerading as the legendary headless horseman.

Isaac Johnson was among the first to arrive and the first to die in the Boston colony, and as Hawthorne notes, his property became the site for the graveyard and prison.

Lethe is a river in the underworld of Greek and Roman myth. A drink from it makes the taster forget everything. In *Paradise Lost,* the fallen angels are forever trying to reach this river to alleviate their torments.

Loco-foco is originally a self-lighting cigar or match, but it came to be applied to a faction of the Democratic party called the Equal Rights Party, and still later it was an abusive term used by the Whigs for all Democrats. Its use in the "Custom House" section by Hawthorne for himself is another instance of the whimsy which acts as an ironic prelude to the sorrows and anquish in the following chapters.

Lord of Misrule or *master of revels* is the rough and ready equivalent of the master of ceremonies in medieval Christmas festivities. The Lord was usually aided in his pranks by youngsters. Pearl is likened to one of these assistants.

Martin Luther (1483—1546), son of a miner, and later lecturer at the University of Wittenberg, was the fiery father of the Reformation in Germany. Luther was shocked at the means used by the religious to raise money for the Church at Rome, and these abuses and others, as well as his zealous disposition, led him to write his well-known ninety-five theses about indulgences and papal perrogatives in 1517. In 1520, he published his "Address to the Christian Nobles of Germany" and *On the Babylonish Captivity of the Church* which further questioned and disputed the doctrinal system of the Catholic Church. During a year of protective seclusion at Wartburg, he translated the Bible into German and wrote several other treatises. His more well-known works of general interest are *Table Talk, Letters,* and his *Sermons.* Although Luther had a rather coarse sense of humor and at times an ill-tempered disposition, he had a vivid and electrifying mind, one which could fire the imagination of common folk and nobility alike. His hymns are good examples of his bold and rugged power of expression.

Increase Mather (1639—1723), son of Richard and father to Cotton, was a famous American divine who was president of Harvard College (1685—1701). He was far less an alarmist over the supposed presence of witches than his son, and his *Cause of Conscience Concerning Witchcraft* (1693) did much to calm the fears of that threat among New Englanders.

Matthew, the evangelist, was a tax collector when Christ called him to the ministry: "As Jesus passed on from there, he saw a man called Matthew sitting at the tax office; and he said to him, 'Follow me.' And he rose and followed him" (Matthew ix, 9). The oldsters at the Salem custom station are far too debilitated to receive a human, much less divine, commission.

General James F. Miller, as Hawthorne mentions in "The Custom House," had held the post of Collector of Customs; he had fought bravely in the 1812 war with the English.

Nepenthe, like the waters of the River Lethe, was a drug supposed by the ancient Greeks to cause permanent forgetfulness of sorrow.

New Jerusalem is the "Heavenly City" for the redeemed, those "who walk with God on earth;" see Revelation xxi, 2.

Nightshade (belladona) and *Henbane* are flowering plants related to the tomato and potato, the juice of which is poisonous; in folklore the plants are believed to have some magical effect, usually for the bad.

Sir Thomas Overbury (1581—1613) had opposed the marriage of his friend and patron Robert Carr, the Viscount Rochester, to Carr's mistress, Frances Howard, Countess of Essex. Lady Essex conspired to have Overbury imprisoned in the Tower of London and there poisoned. Three months later, Carr and Frances Howard were married. Statements in the posthumous letters of one Doctor Simon Forman, astrologer and peddler of love potions, implicated that not-so-good doctor in the machinations of the Countess. Overbury is remembered, not for his unfortunate court life, but for his *Characters* (1614) which are quick and witty portraits of types of people.

Paracelsus was the self-coined name of Theophrastus Bombastus von Hohenheim (1493—1541), the son of a Swiss physician. He acquired fame as a medical doctor in his own right, and was appointed town physician of Basel in 1526. His arrogance and intemperance caused him to leave that post a few years later. Although he was attracted to alchemy and quack mysticism, he was a learned man and helped improve pharmacy and various medical methods, and made new chemical compounds. In linking his name with this scientist, Chillingworth shows the scientific duality of his own knowledge; Chillingworth is a learned scientist, and proves as much by curing Hester and her child in prison, but he also is attracted to the weird and unwholesome as was the Swiss doctor.

Pearl has several important meanings in early literature. St. Matthew (xiii, 45—46), speaking of the kingdom of heaven, says that "it is like a merchant in search of fine pearls, who, on finding one pearl of great value, went and sold all that he had and bought it." This is the reference that Hawthorne is using in Chapter VI. In an anonymous medieval allegory by that name, the pearl is a lost girl sought by her father; he finds out that she has become a bride of Christ, meaning possibly that she has taken the veil, that she has died to the pleasures of this world, or that she has entered heaven. The dual nature of Hester's Pearl is carried by this religious association of her name and by references to the girl's elfin and seemingly demonic disposition. She is certainly not of Salem's religious world, but she is precious and good in her own right.

Pequots was a tribe in the Algonquian nation who lived in east
necticut. As Hawthorne suggests, the tribe had been finally
by British and colonial forces.

P.P., Clerk of this Parish is a literary allusion to the *Memoirs of P.P.,*
of This Parish, an 18th century pseudo-autobiography, which parod
the life stories of English gentry and religious who tried to immortaliz
themselves with tedious and tepid skill. Hawthorne is jokingly deriding
his own attempts at telling of his life at the customs house.

Protectorate is the designation given that period of English history (1653—
1658) when Oliver Cromwell, the great Puritan military leader, ruled
as head of state. He did his best to establish a commonwealth in
England, and it would have taken quick root had he lived longer.
However, in less than two years after his death, the nation was again
a monarchy.

Jonathan Pue is mentioned in Joseph Felt's *Annals of Salem* as having been
a surveyor of Customs in the 18th century. It is supposedly from research done by Pue that Hawthorne "discovers" the story of *The Scar-*
let Letter.

William Shirley, and English-born lawyer, served as Governor in Massachusetts in the periods 1740—1749 and 1753—1756.

General Zachary Taylor (1784—1850), twelfth President of the United States,
was elected on the Whig ticket in 1848; his election, with its changes
in patronage, led to Hawthorne losing his customs post and gave the
author pause to write *The Scarlet Letter* as is mentioned in "The Custom House" section.

Tongues of Flame, see Acts ii, 1-11. The Holy Spirit visited the disciples
of Christ after His death and gave them power to speak so as to be
understood by anyone listening.

The Town Pump, or more properly, "A Rill from the Town Pump," is a
section in Hawthorne's *Twice Told Tales* (1837); it describes the ordinary life in Salem.

Utopia, meaning "not a place" or nowhere, is the word commonly used
to designate the ideal state where there is no want and all are satisfied.
Hawthorne used the term in Chapter I where he describes the prison
at Salem. There, as elsewhere in the work when similar allusions are

Hawthorne is making an ironic commentary on how far
als in the new world have departed from the optimism of
ng-out; they have brought a sense of evil into what they had
_o_ be a second Eden, a Utopia, and as a consequence cannot
_or_ tranquility. The only thing new about the new world is the
aphy. Sir Thomas More's _Utopia_ (1515) was familiar to the set-
_s_ as a commentary on the imperfections of the England they had
_t._ Hawthorne was undoubtedly thinking of this work and its repu-
ation among the colonials when he used the word; they have left
England but not its imperfections.

Wapping is an early wharf-site in London.

John Wilson (1591—1667) was an English Congregational minister who
came to the Massachusetts colony in 1630. The description that
Hawthorne gives of this man in Chapter III is partly interpretive, but
in general outline agrees with his reputation and the comments made
later by Cotton Mather, a famous American divine, in his _Magnalia
Christi._

John Winthrop (1588—1649) was born in Suffolk, England. He left the law
to assume governorship of the Massachusetts Bay Colony in 1630. He
was re-elected governor with brief intervals up to his death. During
his active life in the New World, he, more than any other person, did
the most to form and direct the political institutions in the northern
colonies. The first part of his _Journal_ was published in 1790; it is an
extremely valuable history of the Massachusetts colony. His oldest son,
John, was governor of Connecticut and founded the town of New
London in 1646. Winthrop's grandson, John, was governor of the Connecticut colony in 1698.

Witches' Sabbath is a gathering of witches, warlocks, and others devoted to
Satan to worship that fallen angel and his evil power. In her frequent
and mysterious trips to the forest, Mistress Hibbins is said to participate in such rites. A service of this kind is described in Hawthorne's
short story, "Young Goodman Brown."